THE REAL DEADWOOD

TRUE LIFE HISTORIES OF WILD BILL HICKOK, CALAMITY JANE, OUTLAW TOWNS, AND OTHER CHARACTERS OF THE LAWLESS WEST

JOHN AMES

Chamberlain Bros.
a member of Penguin Group (USA) Inc.
New York

Chamberlain Bros.
a member of
Penguin Group (USA) Inc.
375 Hudson Street
New York, NY 10014

An application has been submitted to register this book with the
Library of Congress.

ISBN 1-59609-031-6

Printed in the United States of America

20 19 18 17 16 15 14 13 12

Book designed by Mike Rivilis.

CONTENTS

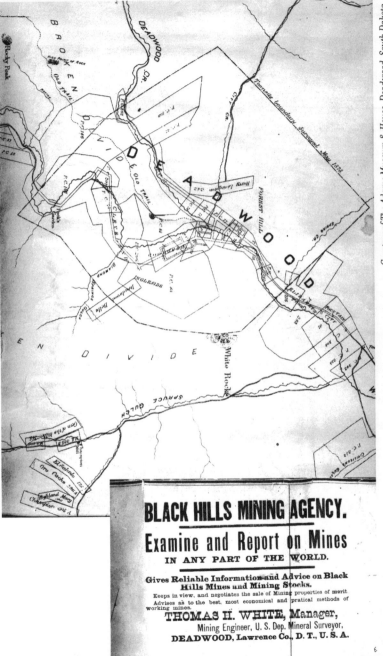

BLACK HILLS MINING AGENCY.

Examine and Report on Mines
IN ANY PART OF THE WORLD.

Gives Reliable Information and Advice on Black
Hills Mines and Mining Stocks.

Keeps in view, and negotiates the sale of Mining properties of merit.
Advises as to the best, most economical and pratical methods of
working mines.

THOMAS H. WHITE, Manager,
Mining Engineer, U. S. Dep. Mineral Surveyor,
DEADWOOD, Lawrence Co., D. T., U. S. A.

CHAPTER ONE

"POOR MAN'S DIGGINGS!" THE BIRTH OF DEADWOOD

"It was not part of America," *Deadwood* series creator David Milch says about the infamous goldstrike camp that became a literally illegal town. "They were an outlaw community, and they knew it."

Present-day Deadwood, South Dakota, is the seat of Lawrence County, located in the western part of the state in the northern tip of the verdant, wildlife-teeming Black Hills. Despite devastating fires, floods, mud slides, epidemics, blizzards, and several economic crises, Deadwood's tenacious residents have not only endured, they've triumphed. Today, with the twin lures of their carefully preserved past and eighty gambling establishments, this town of not quite fourteen-hundred residents manages to entice two million visitors a year.

It's an unlikely fate for a community born of violence and blatant trespass on Lakota Sioux land. Just how might that early Deadwood of 1875-76 stack up against Tombstone, Abilene, Dodge, Hays City, and other notorious "hellers" in the pantheon of Wild West towns?

Plenty of towns in the Old West were violent in the two decades following the Civil War. Texas towns were all known for being rough as bore bristles, especially Fort Griffin (ruins now), Laredo, San Antonio, and El Paso. Independence, Missouri, was a wild frontier settlement where Wild Bill fought the first ever "walking showdown," and Cimarron, New Mexico, was a favorite place to unlimber for killers like Clay Allison.

The 1870s cow towns (railroad towns surrounded by "graze" and equipped with extensive cattle pens) were the last stop along the famous long-drive trails originating in the longhorn cattle country of southeast Texas. Most earned reputations for being rough and wide-open: Sedalia, Abilene, and Ellsworth on the Missouri-Pacific and Kansas-Pacific railroads; Dodge City on the Atchison, Topeka and Santa Fe Railroad. Drunk cowboys cutting up roughshod at anything in sight. Railroad brakemen, approaching cattle railheads at night, always hastened to blow out their lanterns—favorite targets of inebriated cow nurses.

The concentration of money in cow towns drew gamblers, thieves, "soiled doves" (prostitutes), flimflam artists—and killers, both the professional and the impulsive amateur. The gunfighter was a product of the Civil War and its brutal lessons in "easy-go killing."

Among all the cow towns, James Butler "Wild Bill" Hickok once opined, Abilene was the toughest of the bunch. And as one of the few men to succeed in taming that clapboard hellhole, albeit briefly, he likely knew. One night in Abilene, the lead flew so fast and furious that Marshal Hickok accidentally "powder-burned" his own deputy into an early grave.

But, then again, Hickok survived Abilene; he wouldn't be so lucky a few years later in Deadwood.

No matter how wide-open those early cow towns might have been, historians and frontier buffs alike agree: there was no hellhole quite as hellish as a gold-strike camp. "[Wyatt] Earp said gunmen in Deadwood were as proficient as in any western community, except possibly Tombstone." And both were gold-strike towns.

Most of the men were there for one reason: to locate "color." And often, whatever gold they found they kept on their person. Gold-strike camps were sometimes visited by silent "bedroll killers," murdering thieves who slashed the throats, or caved in the skulls, of sleeping and drunk prospectors.

In the early Black Hills gold rush days, such killings were rarely investigated, in part because they were usually attributed to Indians—the favorite scapegoat of early Black Hills murderers. As is the case with the massacre of white settlers, killed at Al Swearengen's order, in the Pilot—episode 1 of HBO's Deadwood.

Just how deadly was Deadwood in those fledgling years? Milch quantified the point starkly during an

HBO press session for the show. Deadwood's average of one and a half murders a day, he pointed out, equaled about ten percent of the population per year. Such a murder rate in modern New York City would mean 700,000 New Yorkers killed annually.

But even this astounding risk was no deterrent for desperate men lured by the euphoric shout, "Poor man's diggings!" That was the magnetic pull of Deadwood Gulch and the Black Hills: easy placer gold. Gold found in relatively shallow deposits of gravel and sand, so that no expensive equipment or elaborate mining was required to get at it. And, for quite a few, the promise panned out: a million dollars' worth of gold (at $20 an ounce) was pulled out in just June and July of 1876—perhaps a bit of it by Wild Bill, who told his wife he did a little prospecting during the three weeks or so he spent in Deadwood.

"THE RICHEST 100 SQUARE MILES ON EARTH": THE BLACK HILLS

The Lakota called them the Paha Sapa, whites called them the Black Hills (from a distance, they often appear dark even at high noon). By any name, this beautiful, mysterious, isolated extension of the Rocky Mountains is a perfect backdrop for the almost surreal place that early Deadwood must have seemed.

The Black Hills are a high-altitude island of timber surrounded by level, barren, treeless plain. They are far less arid than the surrounding region because some of the peaks rise more than a mile high. Thus, they arrest rain clouds that otherwise quickly blow over the dry plains. The resulting forests and streams make the Black Hills a haven for bears and other wildlife.

Forested slopes are covered with tall ponderosa pine, spruce, and aspen. Here and there, as travelers move through, huge chunks of crystallized gypsum flash like mirrors in the sunlight. Ancient granite peaks have been wind-eroded to spires. Limestone formations dot the region. Caves honeycomb the hills, and entire streams sometimes disappear underground.

But the Black Hills is also a weatherworn place that easily yields its secrets to inquiring eyes. The domelike "uplift" of the Black Hills, combined with long centuries of erosion, have laid bare the subsurface areas. Nothing proves this more graphically than the tilting, fully exposed strata of the "Deadwood formation," as geologists call the impressive cliff above the town of Deadwood—a cliff shaped very much like the one from which Dan Dority tosses Brom Garret in Episode 3, "Reconnoitering the Rim."

A place that so openly beckons to gold-hungry men will always get "noised about." Almost from the first moment white men laid eyes on the Black Hills, gold was their chief interest in the place (although a few brave or foolish fur trappers, too, sometimes risked angering the highly territorial Lakota).

An early Jesuit missionary hinted he had seen evidence of gold there. A reported strike in 1834 ended in disaster with the Lakota killing all the miners. Another party in 1852 found gold, but had to flee before taking any out.

The Lakota Sioux did not "own" the Paha Sapa in the strictly legal sense, only by right of squatter's claim. But the U.S. government chose to formally recognize that claim in 1868 (the Treaty of Fort Laramie) and declared the Black Hills part of the Great Sioux Reservation. It was off-limits to whites, and the Lakota were determined to make sure the "talking paper" was upheld.

Needless to say, the white frontier settlers had a vastly different view of things than did eastern politicians or the Lakota, who viewed gold as simply "the glittering yellow rocks," not a dream come true. Various promoters, such as Charles Collins of Sioux City, not only kept the gold fever alive but organized expeditions into the Black Hills.

At first, the U.S. Army made some effort at good faith with the Sioux, forcing these trespassers off the ceded lands. But clearly some within government (perhaps with a newfound "glitter" in their own eyes?) were growing more ambivalent about their recent promise to the Lakota (the Lakota, too, violated the treaty by attacking railroad workers and others). In 1874, George Armstrong Custer commanded a government-sponsored expedition that confirmed the rumors: There was indeed gold in them thar Black Hills.

Various sources note that the U.S. government, in an effort to honor the Treaty of Fort Laramie, tried to conceal the discovery from the general public. If so, they would have had better luck trying to hold the ocean back with a broom. Especially with "Iron Butt" Custer among the promoters, busting his brevet to create a gold stampede into the Black Hills.

"Men without former experience in mining," Custer wrote in August 1874, "have discovered it [gold] at the expense of but little time and labor."

Translation: "Poor man's diggings!" And so it began: white trespassers flooding along "Freedom's Trail," as they called the route Custer blazed for them. The Lakota called it "Thieves' Road." By 1876, illegal whites were ten thousand strong in the Black Hills. Deadwood Gulch (which takes its name from all the dead trees that once lined the walls of the narrow canyon) was heading toward a population of about five thousand—almost four times its present number.

Like toadstools after a hard rain, Deadwood, Rapid City, and Lead (pronounced leed, Deadwood's "Twin City") popped into existence in the northern region of the Black Hills. By January 1876, cabins, shanties, and tents flourished along Deadwood and Whitewood creeks and in surrounding areas. One of those original claims, the Homestake (1876-2001), went on to become the Western Hemisphere's richest source of gold: 2.7 million tons in its 125 years of production.

PANIC ON THE PLAINS

Who were these original "sooners" who founded an illegal, lawless town belonging to no nation?

They were almost all males, at first, with a male-female ratio of about 200 to 1, which was par for the course on the frontier. And many of them were destitute family men who were among the first to have been defeated by the Great Plains.

Not until after the Civil War did whites try to settle the Great Plains in any large numbers. Even well into the 1860s, maps and globes still labeled this region the "Great American Desert."

America began in the woodlands, and only slowly did we venture out of them. The Great Plains were so foreign to the pioneer experience that the Oregon migration of the 1840s was from one wooded region to another. The Plains weren't even considered for settlement despite being more fertile, in places, than the Pacific Coast. Walter Prescott Webb called this "an example of a frontier jumping nearly two thousand miles over an unoccupied country."

After the war, however, railroads began a vigorous campaign to lure Americans, and especially naive immigrants, to the Plains. "Rain follows the plow!" insisted advertisements, promoting the widely accepted (and remarkable silly) belief that merely cultivating the soil would somehow stimulate rainfall.

The cyclical nature of drought, on the Great Plains, was not understood yet. If it rained last summer, then the rationale was that surely it would rain this summer too. But while the Black Hills form an oasis, the Plains around them can, at times, be like a desert—and worse. In 1874, the year preceding the stampede into the Black Hills and Deadwood, one of the worst grasshopper plagues in U.S. history wiped out the Great Plains wheat crop.

Also fresh on the minds of those early "sooners" (people who occupy homestead land before it's legally available) was the Panic, or depression, of 1873. On September 18 of that year, Jay Cooke & Company, a New York banking firm, closed their doors. This triggered the first full-blown panic among cattlemen.

Cattle prices fell so low they didn't even cover the cost of shipping the beef back east. And if the cattle barons were suffering, everyone out west suffered. Prices for farm crops plunged, too, and stayed low.

Money was tight, jobs were scarce (one of the most popular new songs of the 1870s was "Out of Work"). So those sooners arrived in Deadwood with two basic goals in mind: to work hard by day, and raise hell by night. And in old Deadwood they didn't just raise hell, Pilgrim, they tilted it a few feet.

CHAPTER TWO

ENTERING THE BADLANDS:
AL SWEARENGEN
AND THE GEM

I t's widely reported that a parade greeted the arrival of Wild Bill Hickok and Charlie Utter's wagon train in Deadwood in July 1876. But all those cheering men weren't welcoming Hickok. They were hooraying the arrival of Deadwood's first batch of whores, who were traveling in Hickok's party.

After all, this was hardly your typical godfearing community, despite the good efforts of Preacher Smith. Deadwood's very first building was a saloon. And not long after the first saloons came the first "theaters." Among the many of ill repute, none has earned a more florid reputation than the Gem Theater/Saloon and its real-life owner, Al Swearengen.

"This notorious den of iniquity," Black Hills pioneer John S. McClintock called the Gem, and he was no blue nose. As for *Deadwood* villain Al Swearengen (Ian McShane), the true behavior of real-life Swearengen in real-life Deadwood suggests the HBO series has aptly portrayed this psychopathic profiteer.

Not only were Swearengen and the Gem real, so were Dan Dority (general manager of the Gem, played by W. Earl Brown) and Johnny Burnes (floor manager and in charge of the girls, played by Sean Bridgers with the last name simplified to "Burns"). From all accounts, the real Al Swearengen and his lickspittles were remarkably similar to the series snakes.

Right down to the controversial cussing. "*Deadwood* . . . has more dirty words in its first 15 minutes than two or three hours worth of *The Sopranos*," wrote Tom Shales in the *Washington Post*. Another critic called it a "mud-, blood- and vulgarity-soaked Western." Some even think the cussing "approaches self-parody," especially Al Swearengen's foul mouth.

The Gem Theatre (Al Swearengen is said to be in the wagon on the left). Courtesy of The Adams Museum & House, Deadwood, South Dakota.

But history has recently vindicated art. In the April 23, 2004, Rapid City Journal, staff writer Denise Ross reported on the recent find of an 1880 letter (located near Swearengen's home on Forest Avenue) written by Swearengen's second wife, Emmie, to her mother.

"It said how profane he was and that he was mean to her," said Mary Kopco, director of Deadwood's Adams Memorial Museum.

Swearengen's first wife, Nettie, had already divorced him for abuse.

Little is known about Al Swearengen's life before he arrived in Deadwood except that he probably came from Chicago and was likely part of the gold rush from Custer (located in the Black Hills due south of Deadwood). He's depicted as being of some British decent in the HBO series, but only because McShane is.

But according to Deadwood historians, there's little doubt that he ran a white slave operation in the Gem. He enticed women from the States (South Dakota was part of the Dakota Territory then) with the lure of respectable employment. After they arrived, they were stranded, scared, and helpless, and many did not speak English. The alternative was the street—and for a woman in all-male, lawless Deadwood, that meant no alternative at all.

Once trapped by Swearengen, the women could not turn to the law—there wasn't any. In fact, Deadwood's criminals were brazenly open about their nefarious deeds in 1876. No doubt one reason Swearengen could risk such blatantly criminal behavior was the fact that, technically, he couldn't be breaking U.S. laws on sovereign Indian land. Seth Bullock couldn't stand Swearengen and his operation. *Deadwood* producer Scott Stephens notes that the two men literally drew a line on Main Street separating the red-light district, under Swearengen's control, from the part Bullock and the law controlled. Swearengen ruled his own territory.

As a result, "the Gem had the reputation for the most vile entertainment and debasement of women who were pressed into service." The staff (which, not surprisingly, included several bouncers) were reportedly as nasty as Swearengen, and the women were routinely beaten and humiliated.

The Gem, which opened in June 1876, the month before Hickok arrived, was only one of many "theaters" in Deadwood. Some really were legitimate theaters; others, like the Gem, the Melodeon, the Green Front, and the Bella Union across the street, as it is in the series, were brothels offering coarse skits. However, Swearengen sometimes "brought in amazing performers—actors, singers, vaudeville acts—to do legitimate theater," Kopco said.

A famous 1876 photo of Main Street in Deadwood shows a town already well built up while also still building. The street looks more like a muddy buffalo wallow than a thoroughfare and seems completely blocked by building materials. But the first saloons and theaters are visible, including the Gem—a collection of rectangular frame buildings, mostly two

Main Street in Deadwood, 1876. Courtesy of The Adams Museum & House, Deadwood, South Dakota.

or three stories, with false fronts. More functional than fancy, as was much of the frontier West.

This collection of disreputable establishments, concentrated on Lower Main at the north end of town, became known as "the Badlands." (This original Deadwood existed for only three years—the great fire of 1879 gutted the business area.) And whether it was called a saloon, a theater, or a gambling house, eventually most establishments "ran a string of whores topside."

Armed and dangerous outlaws prowled the streets of Deadwood, unchallenged, and stepping into the Gem could buy you even more trouble. Yet, despite Swearengen's greed and brutality, the Gem was the going place in town. According to the Adams Museum, on a typical night Swearengen took in $5,000—and some nights the take reached $10,000. Those amounts were huge in 1876, when a typical family might have to survive on about $600 dollars or less annually.

In one episode of *Deadwood*, Calamity Jane (Robin Weigert) refers to Swearengen as "the Slimy Limy."

But the real-life Calamity logged plenty of hours at the Gem, where she was treated as a popular celebrity. Some researchers say it's possible, others probable, that Calamity worked as a prostitute in Deadwood (but there's no proof), and quite possible that she even procured girls for Swearengen before briefly running her own house.

NIGHT LIFE IN DEADWOOD

Early Deadwood was grimly masculine (two hundred males for every female), and, for many, work went on "from can to can't." And once work was over, it was time to cut the wolf loose.

By 1877, Deadwood was home to about seventy-five establishments calling themselves saloons. There were dozens more vice parlors billing themselves as theaters or gambling houses. Deadwood residents boasted that no other town its size could even compete in the hell-raising department.

It wasn't just Deadwood Gulch that supplied customers to the incredible number of honky-tonks that sprang up in Deadwood—there were camps all

Inside the Gem Theatre, where "happy hour" featured gambling, prostitution, dancing, and drinking. Courtesy of The Adams Museum & House, Deadwood, South Dakota.

over the area, including at Custer and Hill City. As many as ten thousand men may have crowded into the town in its heyday, many from the surrounding slopes that were rapidly "peopling up." They were overwhelmingly male, young and restless —and horny as a Texas toad, especially after tossing back a few jolts of Who-Shot-John, usually taken neat.

But Swearengen and other proprietors in the Badlands seldom relied on whores alone. Their goal was to separate the miners from as much of their gold as possible, by any means they could get away with.

In the gambling houses and saloons like the No. 10 (Deadwood had so many it was easier to just number them), draw poker was preferred among professional gamblers. Most saloons ran two kinds of poker action: a penny-ante game called "joker poker," and the serious game for winners of joker poker. But faro was more profitable for the house and more attractive to amateurs. In this card game, popular throughout the nineteenth century, a player bets against the bank as to which card will be chosen from a dealer's box.

Ideally, the proprietor hired an attractive female to run "the faro rig." The chance to sit down at a table, and gaze at a quality female, was usually a bigger lure than the fun of wagering.

And wagering was at the very heart of having fun on the frontier. Bare-knuckle boxing was in vogue because it offered both a show and a wager on the outcome. Likewise cockfighting (still legal in New Mexico and Louisiana), dogfighting, and "ratting"—a lively event, no doubt, in which a dog or weasel was sicced on live rats and bets were placed on how many rats would be killed in a specified amount of time.

Craps, which began as a dice game called "crabs" in New Orleans, was played in every region of the country by the 1870s. Other popular games of chance included roulette, monte (a variation of faro), and keno (similar to bingo). Billiards, too, was a game both enjoyable and rife with betting opportunities.

The mostly crude theatrical fare at the Badlands establishments wasn't for everyone. Legitimate businesses such as Jack Langrishe's theater, the Deadwood Opera House, and Nye's Theater offered drama and opera. But it was the Badlands that housed the greatest lure of all: female flesh.

DEADWOOD'S SIREN SONG

If you'd like some idea just how important prostitution was in Deadwood, consider this: It took decades, and the combined might of the feds, South Dakota state officials, and local law enforcement, to finally shut down Deadwood's four remaining brothels—the last in

1980! Prostitution remained legal (with brief interruptions) for more than a century.

The fact is really not all that shocking. Even in the way back days, America was never as prudish as many people now believe. For example, a study of records kept in 1790s New England revealed that one-third of all brides were pregnant at the time of marriage.

Pregnancy was only one of the risks that prostitutes (soiled doves, or "sporting girls") faced. There was also the risk of STDs (sexually transmitted diseases), physical abuse from customers and the hired help, and an alarmingly high suicide rate. The working life of a typical frontier prostitute was only a few years.

Contraception was fairly well understood by the 1870s (the birthrate fell from slightly over 7 children per couple in 1800 to only 4.24 by 1880). But the methods were notoriously unreliable. Condoms made from the lining of sheep intestines were available in the 1700s. They were not preformed to fit the man's penis, but rather, simply shaped like a handkerchief and held in place during the act. James Boswell, Dr. Johnson's biographer, complains bitterly about them in his comically frank London Journal.

Worse, they cost $1 apiece (around $25 today), which usually meant they were washed and used over. Because of their pleasure-robbing thickness, they were more commonly used in England and Europe than in the U.S. Particularly in frontier whorehouses, American males insisted on "riding bareback."

Thus, the onerous reality of birth control fell to the woman. One device in widespread use was a contraceptive sponge with a thread attached so the sponge could be easily removed. Another method was douching with spermicides such as alum or zinc sulfate. "Female syringes" were sold for this purpose.

Perhaps most widely used was the pessary, or "pisser," a precursor of the modern diaphragm. Made of wood, cotton, or sponge, the pessary was sold as a medical device for "correcting a prolapsed [out of place] uterus." But most women knew its real purpose even if men never caught on.

These methods varied in their effectiveness. But given the frequency of intercourse (a former Deadwood prostitute reported servicing twenty-eight men in one night), failures were common. Which might help explain why one in six pregnancies was aborted by the 1860s.

By the time Deadwood Gulch filled up, at least twenty-five different chemical abortifacients were widely available and openly sold under such euphemistic names as "infallible French female pills." Marc McCutcheon notes that surgical abortion was available by 1861 and cost $10 to $100. Unfortunately, many surgeons of that day still scoffed at Joseph Lister's insistence on the importance of disinfecting operating rooms and surgical equipment (more on this later) and many women died of postoperative infections.

The Gem was an especially rough place for a prostitute because of the way Swearengen set it up for high-volume business. Deadwood's Adams Museum web site (see "Books and Web Sites for Further Reading" on page TK) describes the place as "a two story building, 30 feet wide by 100 feet long . . . The rear of the building was divided up into small rooms where Swearengen's girls entertained customers."

Small rooms out back . . . in other words, Swearengen's operation was so crude the men were serviced in bare "cribs" instead of the lacy, feminine, upstairs rooms of a high-class brothel. This saved time and allowed floor manager Johnny Burnes to keep a close eye on things. It no doubt also forced the women to be with more men each night.

Given the secret nature of prostitution, there is no record of what men actually paid for a "short time." But in her Deadwood Magazine series "Girls of the Gulch," Rena Webb estimated (based on prices for other goods and services) the going rate was at least $1.50, quite likely a bit higher.

Payment was most often in gold dust, either weighed on a scale or (more likely) taken as a "pinch" from a prospector's gold sack (weighing dust was time-consuming).

Many of these men were of course drunk, and it was not uncommon for them to have their pockets picked while they were blissfully distracted in the poorly lighted crib. The soiled doves were not usually the actual thieves—that job often fell to a "panel thief" working for the proprietor.

Panel-thieving was as simple as it was effective. The victim was instructed to leave his clothing on a chair placed close to a wall. But it was a fake wall equipped with a well-hidden panel that slid quickly and silently back and forth. All it took was a minute or two to slide the panel back, rifle through the victim's pockets, then shut the panel again.

It should be noted that not all prostitutes in early Deadwood were managed by pimps like Swearengen. There also had to be free agents because, in 1878, the Deadwood Times was pushing for a tax on all prostitutes not working in brothels. Perhaps Swearengen and company were behind that campaign?

"A BALL OF DOPE" AND DEADWOOD'S CHINATOWN

No discussion of night life in Deadwood would be complete without mentioning the town's Chinese community, which numbered around four hundred residents at its peak.

Pete Dexter's critically acclaimed novel *Deadwood* (1986), which depicts Wild Bill's fatal sojourn in

Deadwood, includes scenes in a Chinese opium den. So does the 1995 movie *Wild Bill*, directed by Walter Hill and adapted from Dexter's book. Hill also directed the pilot for HBO's *Deadwood*, and, presumably, "the ball of dope" Swearengen keeps alluding to is opium in the sticky, tarlike form then available in Chinese opium dens.

But this is probably creative license on the part of the writers, because, in 1876, when Hickok was still alive, Deadwood's Chinatown hadn't yet taken shape— not until the 1880s. However, it's not much of a stretch because there were Chinese in Deadwood. Enough, by 1878, that some miners felt compelled to form the Caucasian League to protect their interests.

The idea that the Chinese were needed to support an opium addiction in the 1870s is laughable. Their support wasn't needed—hundreds of thousands of Americans were addicted because narcotics simply weren't yet controlled by law (not until 1914). Opium was openly sold in drugstores throughout the country. It was available as pills or as laudanum, which was opium with alcohol—the lady's choice, as addict Alma

Garret (Molly Parker) symbolizes. After the Civil War, morphine was also widely available.

It's true that Deadwood's Chinatown (gone now but once located near the Badlands) included opium dens and brothels. But most of the Chinese ran legitimate businesses or worked hard sifting through ore tailings in abandoned gold mines (by law, the Chinese could not work any new digs, only those abandoned by whites). They were so self-sufficient that they even had their own fire department, police force, and mayor.

However, the Chinese represented something that scared many Americans: cheap labor. On the railroads, they were paid $32.50 per month versus the $52 paid to whites. This fear of wage sabotage, coupled with loss of mining jobs and increasing pressure to shut down opium dens and brothels, chipped away at Chinatown. Ching Ong, the last Chinese resident of Deadwood, left in 1931.

CHAPTER THREE

PANNING FOR COLOR

"Gone to bury my wife; be back in half an hour," read a note on the door of a prospector's shack in the 1860s, pretty much saying all that needs to be said about gold fever.

Probably very few of those early Black Hills pioneers knew the technical word "aggradation." But that's the process that helped so many of them find gold with just simple tools like a pickax, a rake, and a pan. Placer gold, just like the easy pickings that characterized the California gold rush of '49.

In the East, streams tend to erode. In the West, they tend to aggrade; that is, to raise the level of the streambed by depositing sediment. And among those deposits is gold. The Black Hills teems with aggrading

Gold miners operate a ground sluice near Deadwood. (Denver Public Library, Western History Collection, X-61151).

water streams. Geologically, there's also the hills' natural "uplift event" that exposed so many subsurface regions to plain view. (And makes it entirely plausible that Dan Dority, in episode 3 of *Deadwood*, could simply "spot" a rich gold vein in a cliff face.)

Sooners quickly learned where to look for gold. Streams, such as Deadwood Creek, emerging from a range of mountains or hills form an apron of deposits, beginning at the base of the mountains or hills. "Placers" are deposits of sand and gravel containing valuable minerals. Other good spots to find placers are anywhere the current slackens—bends or holes in the streambed or behind boulders. Also, the annual "summer shrink" of waterways out west exposes "bars," deposits of gold-bearing gravel.

Placer gold . . . poor man's diggings. Most of the Black Hills Argonauts (in mythology, those who sailed with Jason on the Argo in quest of the Golden Fleece; also refers to gold prospectors) were not well versed in geology or mining technology. They were not deep-rock miners who worked far underground; they would come later and are still mining the hills to this day. The Argonauts worked almost exclusively in streams and rivers, searching for rich placers. And even without formal training, they learned a lot about gold and how and where to find it.

THE SOONERS AND THE SIOUX

The stampede into the Black Hills was the last great gold rush in the continental U.S. In 1875, there were about eight hundred white men mining or living in the Black Hills, according to an estimate by an Army colonel stationed in the area. By 1876, as America celebrated her centennial, that number reached ten thousand. Perhaps not really all that staggering a figure in a nation of about forty million people, many of them poor as Job's turkey.

The Black Hills rush proved again that the gold fever of 1849 had never truly subsided. The strike in California was followed by large strikes in British Columbia (1858), the Comstock Lode in Nevada (1859), and other major strikes in Colorado and present-day Idaho. Sadly, there were also hoaxes and rumors that caused thousands to endure great expense and hardship, all for nothing. Starved for any kind of entertainment, some early prospectors fired gold dust into a hillside and then watched "excited newcomers rush to file their claims," according to Irving Stone in *Men to Match My Mountains*.

There were some real bonanzas, especially for the first ones in, although the twenty-pound "nuggets" found in California seem unique to that place. The first prospectors into Deadwood Gulch worked claims on Deadwood and Whitewood creeks.

There were many European immigrants in the mix, from Ireland, Germany, Czechoslovakia, Norway, Finland, and including a good number from famine-rocked Sweden (the large number of Scandinavians in the area is reflected in the HBO series through Al Swearengen's repeated use of the ethnic slur "squareheads"—a slur also used by the James brothers and Cole Younger's gang when referring to residents of Northfield, Minnesota).

Home was likely a tent, at first, perhaps only a single canvas sheet as a rain shelter. Later, a crude cabin or flimsy shack with a dirt floor. Some made a fortune, but most Argonauts never got rich. Twenty-five to thirty dollars' worth of gold nuggets might be a typical daily average for many. That was equal to about half a month's pay for a working man, so clearly prospecting could be lucrative.

But put yourself in their soggy and ruined shoes. All day long, your feet and legs are in ice-cold water while a sun hotter than the hinges of hell bakes your face, neck, and arms lobster red. Your stomach (more on that shortly) is pinched with hunger, your back feels like it's been hammered hard, and one ear is cocked for the shrill, terrifying sound of eagle-bone whistles —O Jerusalem! The Sioux in battle mode!

After all, they claimed (and still claim today) the hills as their sacred homeland, a claim that was legally upheld by the U.S. Congress in 1868. During 1874, and into '75, the Army kept driving prospectors out. In September '75, the U.S. government offered the Lakota (only their enemies called them Sioux, "snake in the grass") $6 million for their sacred hills. But the Lakota rejected the offer and the Army tossed in the towel. They simply let the gold rush begin in earnest, and Deadwood was born.

HBO's *Deadwood* series opens only two weeks after the defeat (not the "massacre," as it's often erroneously called) of Custer and his storied 7th Cavalry. With the Little Bighorn battlefield a scant 170 miles northwest of Deadwood, it was only logical that the prospectors in Deadwood Gulch and the rest of the Black Hills would expect "Injin trouble."

But their fear remained mostly that—fear. The great Lakota Sioux, and Cheyenne, and Arapaho victory at Little Bighorn marked the beginning of the end for the last "free-ranging Indians" around the Black Hills. Soon after, they were virtual prisoners on reduced reservations.

By 1877, Congress had voted to repeal the 1868 Fort Laramie Treaty. The U.S. took over the Black Hills and forty million additional acres of Lakota land. With the Indian threat thus summarily eliminated, other Black Hills mining camps and towns joined the earlier (1875) camps of Deadwood Gulch, Custer, and Hill City: French Creek (where Custer found gold),

Whitewood Gulch, and Black Tail Gulch.

(This obsessive fondness for using the word "gulch" in naming so many Black Hills gold camps might have been more inspirational than functional. Only a decade earlier, a group of busted and disgusted prospectors in Montana decided to make one last try before giving up. They picked a spot called Last Chance Gulch—and pulled out $20 million in placer gold.)

PANNING, SCAMMING, AND SALT-JUNK BLUES

In the first days of the California gold rush, gold was scratched out of the cracks of rocks with butcher knives. And the Black Hills, too, literally offered easy pickings. Some of the first men in used little equipment; mostly, they just picked up grains of gold with their fingers, occasionally employing the point of a knife.

Eventually, however, the "easy color" got skimmed off, and some equipment was required. And since each miner could file only one claim (which he promptly lost if he stopped actively working it), it was more economical to search a known spot more thoroughly than to give it up and look for new diggings, especially after the choice spots were claimed.

So a typical prospector in the Black Hills was likely to have basic tools to aid his quest: a pickax, a crowbar, a sturdy butcher knife, a shovel, a rake or hoe. If he was a lone operator, he was likely to also have a gold pan. If he had "pards," they might well have advanced to the rocker or even the sluice.

The pan and rocker were primitive, having been in use in Europe since at least the sixteenth century, but extremely helpful to beginners. Pans were both wooden and metal. Frying pans were pressed into service, but a larger pan with flaring sides worked better.

The prospector shoveled in a load of "pay dirt," picked out the pebbles, added water. He then slanted the pan and swished it around until water washed away the earth. With luck, this left "a thread of 'color' in the lowest edge of the dish." David Lavender notes that some men earned a thousand dollars a day employing only a pan.

Sometimes prospectors teamed up, in which case they could improve their take by advancing to a "rocker." Picture a slanted cradle on rockers. It was equipped with a perforated metal sheet that served to screen out the bigger chunks of waste rock. The rest dropped through to the bottom. One man poured in water and shook the cradle, separating the mass. The dirt eventually rinsed out, leaving the gold to settle "behind a series of transverse slats, or riffles."

The problem with both these devices was that they allowed the finer gold dust to escape. Many prospectors didn't care; they could afford a little waste. But some miners (again, especially teams of miners) modified the rocker into a sluice, or "Long Tom." Basically, these were larger, elongated rockers with one scientific improvement: they employed mercury to catch the dust in an amalgam.

But what happened to a claim once it "played out"? If it was abandoned, and no other white man wanted it, then the Chinese were free to work it. But sometimes the temptation posed by gullible, greedy greenhorns was too great, and wily prospectors cashed in by "salting" a claim—planting gold—and then selling their diggings at a good price.

In Leadville, Colorado, "a prospector known as Chicken Bill stole some rich ore from the Little Pittsburgh, dumped it into his own barren shaft, and sold the salted claim to the gullible mayor for one thousand dollars" (The Great West).

Such gullibility was widespread. If anything, gold fever had increased since the days of the forty-niners. That California gold played out just as Europe, then the U.S., went to the gold standard. World markets desperately needed gold, and here in the Black Hills was the answer.

Newspapers and word of mouth wildly exaggerated the opportunities. "Stocks were rising to hundreds of dollars per share in mines where not one dollar in gold or silver had been taken out," notes Stone. Some folks with money to invest, but no common sense about mining, showed up at the goldfields hoping to buy an existing claim. It was child's play to covertly plant a few bright nuggets to catch their eye.

Some of these swindles were too outrageous to

believe, and yet court records prove they worked. One miner planted not only gold but a cut diamond —and sold his claim! Another used the added lure of "fresh fruit" to sell a played out claim. He tied oranges, by small threads, to the branches of some nearby trees. The greenhorns he fleeced had no idea oranges weren't native to the area—or they were too gold-struck to think rationally.

Fresh fruit might seem an odd lure for unloading a worthless claim. But in fact it took an iron stomach to succeed at prospecting. Bad digestion killed far more dreams than bullets or Indians ever did. Food (the lack of it, and its poor quality) was often the prospector's greatest problem.

Hunting was time-consuming and meant time lost from prospecting. Good, fresh, varied foods simply weren't available to most, especially the sooners. The diet was insufficient, monotonous, and loaded with salt.

Many miners lived on biscuits and beans, and Rena Webb (in Deadwood Magazine) has researched the prices they paid in early Deadwood. Flour was usually "$10 for 100 pounds" but it "hit $60" the first winter. A pound of beans was eighteen cents, coffee ran "34 to 38 cents a pound; eggs, 75 cents to a dollar a dozen."

Corn dodgers were easy, quick, and thus widely eaten, especially for breakfast. They were as basic as cornmeal and water, formed into balls and baked in hot ashes. Sometimes bacon, if available, was mixed with them.

Pemmican ("Indian cakes"—lean, dried strips of meat pounded into paste and mixed with fat and berries) and jerked meat stored well and were always appreciated, when available. More common, though, were cured meats called "salt junk" (both of which it was), often pork. Quite common was hardtack, hard, tasteless bread made with only flour and water, and a vile, alkali-tasting concoction called "saleratus bread."

Not only was quality of the food a problem, often the long freighting distances and lack of any "sell by" dates meant that much food was maggot- or weevil infested upon delivery. And often, by necessity, it was eaten that way, the disgruntled diner muttering curses as he tried to eat the good parts, if any. One prospector noted in his journal that he always ate after dark so he couldn't see what he was chewing up.

Even if palatable food was available, the astounding inflation that struck some gold-rich areas sometimes meant that only the wealthy could afford to partake. With so many men desperate for good food, it was a seller's market. At the height of a gold rush, a barrel of flour that normally sold for $20 went as high as $800. Eggs sold for as much as several dollars apiece.

Eventually, however, the surface gold played out and mining corporations moved into the Black Hills. Sadly, yet inevitably, Deadwood's famous but flood-prone creeks (Deadwood and Whitewood) were buried under a four-lane highway in 1967. But still today, scattered throughout the hills, are a few ghost towns—dilapidated legacies of the era when even a poor man could "strike a lode."

CHAPTER FOUR

LAW AND DISORDER
IN DEADWOOD

Three times a day, in modern Deadwood during the summer, "gunslingers" trade insults, then fare off. They move up Main Street from the Badlands to the Franklin Hotel, firing incredibly loud charges that boom throughout the gulch. It's stylized street theater now, but once it was all too real.

"Western gunfights," Ian Frazier wrote in *Great Plains*, "were alcohol-related, or else involved battles over gambling, prostitution, or political preferment. They were closer in spirit to drug wars in the Bronx than to duels of honor."

David Milch's *Deadwood* is neither revisionist nor shocking to those who crave gritty realism and true history of the American frontier. His *Deadwood* is definitely part of the Old West, but not the "guitar-strumming" West of the Hollywood cowboy, pointing the way north to Abilene or Dodge. Early Deadwood was a violent and dangerous place. Brom Garret found out the hard way (in episode 3) that men like Al Swearengen could even get away with murder.

The lawlessness in Deadwood grew more from fear than evil—fear of losing a bonanza in gold. Very early on, Deadwood wasn't just lawless, it was illegal. A white man's town on Indian real estate, and full of gold poachers at that. Swearengen's eagerness to acquit Jack McCall in the HBO series (played by Garret Dillahunt) symbolizes early Deadwood's residents and their fear they might lose a good thing at any moment. Many of those first citizens were reluctant to even report killings for fear the government would run them out.

That said, it's also true the 1870s were ripe for violence and lawlessness on the frontier, the political and social forces in place for conflict and death.

BILLY YANK AND JOHNNY REB
The year 1865 wasn't just the end of the Civil War, it

was also the start of Reconstruction. Federal troops occupied the South for the next twelve years and oversaw changes that, to many white Southerners and even some Yankee sympathizers (known as "copperheads"), were the deliberate destruction of a way of life.

And in fact it was. History had turned the page on the plantation South and slavery. Most Southerners grasped that fact (because most Southerners weren't connected to plantations and only 1 in 6 ever owned a slave). What many of them couldn't easily accept was government-mandated equality for blacks.

Every major advancement for African Americans angered and frightened many Southern whites. In 1867, black males were granted the right to vote in Washington, D.C. Later that same year in Tennessee—cause and effect—the Ku Klux Klan made the transition from a prankster social club to a hostile organization targeting freed slaves, immigrants, and others. In 1875, the Civil Rights Act guaranteed blacks equal access in all public places, including public transportation.

The South (including Texas, where a thousand blacks were lynched during Reconstruction without reprisal) was already angered by ten years of what they considered to be foreign occupation. The region rebelled again, though with "night riders" instead of armies. The Civil Rights Act was simply ignored. Not until the middle of the twentieth century would that 1875 bill finally be enforced.

Obviously, many Southern veterans (and Southerners in general) felt angry and betrayed, felt the Yanks were rubbing it in and gloating, symbolized by the "uppity" carpetbaggers who moved in to profit and meddle. And the Northern vets had every right to resent a bunch of "traitors" who tried to squander George Washington's legacy over the right to keep men in chains. Johnny Reb and Billy Yank, vets or not, clashed often in the aftermath of war, and mining camps like Deadwood Gulch supplied a ready-made tinderbox.

A large number of the early settlers in the Black Hills came from Michigan, Illinois, Minnesota—a region of the country heavily populated by immigrants that was rife with radical politics, including socialism and even communism, as well as the first seeds of what would soon become homegrown populism. Destitute Southerners came north to prospect—conservative, antigovernment types, some even calling themselves "holdout rebels," were suddenly thrown in with the radical, strong federal government crowd. No wonder lead sometimes flew.

The Civil War bred unprecedented carnage and suffering. Many of those veterans on both sides were also afflicted with "soldier's heart"—that era's euphemism for post-traumatic stress disorder. Today, millions of Americans rely on psychopharmacology to help maintain normal behavior. Frontier Americans hadn't yet discovered Prince Valium and his descendants, a point made poignantly clear in *Deadwood*'s portrayal of an emotionally disturbed Calamity Jane.

The logical conclusion is inescapable: there were probably quite a few folks in the West, veterans or not, with various emotional and mental problems that simply went untreated. And in a town like Deadwood, that meant a lot of armed men with impulse control problems.

ROBIN HOOD ROBS 'EM GOOD

One powerful reason for the widespread tolerance of criminals, in Deadwood and the rest of the frontier West, was the "folk hero" mind-set that developed.

Too often, it was easy to romanticize train and bank robbers as victims of "the captains," as some called the wealthy and powerful. Utah-born outlaw Butch Cassidy (Robert LeRoy Parker) was widely known as the "Robin Hood of the West." Texas bank and train robber Sam Bass was lauded as "Robin Hood on a Fast Horse." To this day, California bandit Joaquin Murrietta remains the "Mexican Robin Hood" still honored in ballads despite the fact that "he tied Chinamen [sic] together by their queues, made them dance to the tune of a pistol, then shot their eyes out."

Ironically, one of the nation's great crime fighters—Civil War spy-turned-detective Allan Pinkerton (more on him in chapter 5)—inadvertently contributed to the romanticizing of criminals and crime. In 1875, the same year gold was found on Deadwood Creek, Pinkerton's agents firebombed the James farm in Missouri in a botched effort to nab the famous outlaws, Frank and Jesse. The ill-advised explosion tore off one of their mother's arms and killed their step-brother.

Not the Pinkertons' finest hour. That one bomb hampered law enforcement for years. Widespread national sympathy ensured that the James Gang would be viewed as populist enemies of the railroad men and bankers who victimized the common man.

This Robin Hood stereotype had so thoroughly permeated the national consciousness that Jack McCall, Wild Bill Hickok's killer, relied on it to excuse his cowardly crime. Never a good gambler, McCall played the best card he had: Hey, I'm not a murderer! I killed Hickok because he killed my brother in Abilene, that's all.

The excuse was lame (there was no proof he ever had a brother, and no one had heard about this supposed killing). But in the minds of many, Hickok would always be associated with the vastly unpopular

Scaffold used for hanging the first Indian in Deadwood. (Denver Public Library, Western History Collection, X-31723).

railroads. He was a hero to railroad men at every level because he had shown his typical courage and skill in protecting surveyors and work crews from Indian attacks. Perhaps that association made McCall's flimsy story just good enough. In any event, he was acquitted that first time.

It's more likely, however, that the hokum about Hickok killing McCall's brother was just for public consumption. There was almost surely a different motive behind McCall's acquittal. A journalist of 1876 wrote a long account of the first trial, which was held in the McDaniel's Theater and not the Gem. The piece concludes: "The city is now exceedingly quiet, although people are determined to have no more jury trials."

That's also Al Swearengen's chief concern in HBO's *Deadwood*: "No more of these cocksucking trials." Trials meant publicity, and too much publicity meant a possible end of the boom times. Swearengen seems to symbolize the lawless bad boys of Deadwood, those who had a vested interest in sin and crime.

ROOTS OF DISORDER: BOREDOM, RADICALISM, BIGOTRY

Boredom is an underrated troublemaker. Especially in a place where the stigma of taking a human life is not all that strong. And the blunt truth is that life was cheaper in the frontier West—killing someone was a much bigger deal back in the Land Settled East.

In those heady days, life was an unevenly mixed cocktail of sheer terror and maddening monotony. Violence was, among other things, a temporary escape from that boredom. "Nobody got shot yesterday or last night," mourned the Black Hills Daily Times in May 1878. "It's getting dull."

A killing, or even a good dustup, occasioned a great "stirring and to-do." Anything to help pass the time when you weren't working or sleeping. Some in Deadwood read newspapers, of course, and popular magazines of the day included Scientific American, Sporting Times, and Frank Leslie's Popular Monthly, though copies would have been in short supply and probably hoarded. Dime novels appeared in 1860 and were popular with Civil War soldiers, so there were probably a few around Deadwood Gulch.

But a surprising number of people still believed it was unhealthy to read fiction, that it led to daydreaming, feeblemindedness, "concupiscence," and crime. It might have been easy for some of these folks to become overbearingly serious and rigid, further contributing to the disorder. And no doubt some of them turned to radicalism, which provided an outlet for dogmatic types and permeated the West well into the twentieth century.

South Dakota would not become a state until 1889. But the roots of progressive and populist political views emerged earlier in the region in part a result of the hard luck farmers experienced on the Great Plains. "When men suffer," wrote Walter Prescott, "they become politically radical."

Not everyone who came to Deadwood struck the mother lode. And many in that flood of desperate masculinity had lost everything on the plains after being snookered by the railroad claims of "A hoe-man's paradise awaits you!!!" Their bitterness was understandable; it reflected real and deep suffering. Journalist Bill Harlan, himself a descendant of Black

Hills pioneers, alludes to the area's populist-socialist agenda of last century. (In 1894, Deadwood even elected a populist to Congress, newspaperman Freeman Knowles).

It seems odd today, but politically motivated killings were common on the frontier. Contentious issues included free range vs. fenced land, Negro rights, and women's suffrage. Presumably, few Americans today consider this last issue, to let women vote, radical, but at that time the notion was absurd, even dangerous, to many including some women. After all, history shows that black males were allowed to vote before women, black or white, most of whom had to wait until 1920 before they could vote. Yet out west they could vote in the Utah Territory as early as 1870. But not, however, with the popular support of men.

The country's adoption of the gold standard also divided men into factions. It was widely blamed for the economic plight of many, especially among populists and farmers—particularly, of course, failed farmers. Not too surprisingly, those who were extracting gold from Deadwood Gulch had a different view of the new gold standard. Completing Webb's earlier observation: "When they [men] cease to suffer, they favor the existing order."

Bigotry, too, contributed to the lawlessness and disorder in early Deadwood. But it's not accurate to blame ethnic tensions solely on a narrow-minded dislike of foreigners; again, fear factored in the mix. As Abe Lincoln had put it: "There's too many pigs for the teats."

As mentioned, Swearengen's bigotry toward "squareheads" in the series, for example, reflects the high numbers of Scandinavians living in the Black Hills at the time, many of whose descendants still live there today. In 1878, in the real Deadwood, the Caucasian League was formed to counter the increasing influx of Chinese. Some of the ill will toward new arrivals in America was the fear (mostly unfounded) that too many immigrants meant lower wages and increased unemployment.

There were other reasons for the violence and "let 'er rip!" attitude in Deadwood. The Panic of '73, with its devastating impact on the West, created a sense of live for today, tomorrow we lose it all. And then there's the Black Hills itself, "the last wild place in the lower 48 states." The gold stampede only made it wilder.

In any event, those early residents of Deadwood apparently did some soul-searching after the murder of James Butler Hickok. And before long, they pinned a star on their first sheriff, by God, himself an immigrant, the hero of HBO's *Deadwood*, "straight and courageous" Seth Bullock (played by Timothy Olyphant).

CHAPTER FIVE

DEADWOOD'S FIRST SHERIFF: SETH BULLOCK

"Seth Bullock became, and has ever since remained, one of my staunchest and most valued friends," wrote Theodore Roosevelt in his 1913 autobiography.

Teddy's high regard for "Bully" was well earned. Bullock was still in his twenties when he arrived in Deadwood Gulch on August 1, 1876. But the Canadian-born merchant had already been elected to the Montana Territorial Senate, been a deputy and sheriff in Helena, as well as a businessman, an auctioneer, an explorer, and a conservationist who introduced the resolution that prompted the establishment of Yellowstone Park.

History hasn't forgotten this quintessential

pioneer, but pop culture, (with its love affair with bad boys,) has been slow to warm up to an amazing man who in some ways was visionary. Perhaps that's because the gunfighter defined the Old West, whereas Bullock was a harbinger of the modern, professional lawman. When J. B. Hickok wore a star, he stuck to his famous credo, "Shoot first, ask questions later." Bullock got the job done, too, but tended to leave his shooter holstered.

In real life, Seth Bullock and his partner Sol Star (who's discussed in chapter 8) arrived in Deadwood the day before Wild Bill Hickok was murdered in the No. 10 saloon. Deadwood Gulch was so inaccessible at the time that they had to lower their hardware stock into the narrow canyon by rope. The main street was a thick gumbo of mud, night slops, tripes, all of it attracting a shifting black blanket of flies. And if your claim played out, the saloons paid good money for rat catchers.

Despite all of it, and unlike so many others in Deadwood Gulch, Bullock wasn't there to cash in and get out. For the next forty-three years, he remained

Deadwood's first sheriff, Seth Bullock. Courtesy of The Adams Museum & House, Deadwood, South Dakota.

"a strong and steady force, bringing order to a lawless region and setting the foundation stones for the community that endures today."

NUMEROUS HOT HELLHOLES

Seth Bullock, like Wild Bill Hickok, was the product of a political family that shaped a strong sense of right and wrong in him early on. It's widely reported that he was born in 1849, but recent research by Lynn Bunn, a local historian in Bullock's hometown, disclosed a baptismal record birthdate of July 23, 1847, near Windsor, Ontario, across the Detroit River from Detroit, Michigan. His father, George Bullock, was British, a military man very active in local politics; his mother, Agnes Findley, was born in Scotland.

Maybe his father was too much the military man. Seth and he clashed frequently over "his father's strict attitudes concerning discipline." While still an adolescent, Bullock ran away to have adventures in the Wild West. However, his big plans came to naught when he showed up at the home of his older, married sister in the Montana Territory and she sent the errant youth right back to Ontario.

But young Seth had jackrabbits in his socks, and the second time he came to America it was for good. It was 1867 and he selected Helena, wasting no time in establishing himself there. He first ran for the Senate as a Republican at twenty but lost. He ran again four years later and became a senator at twenty-four years of age. By the time he was twenty-six, he was a county sheriff and chief engineer of the Helena Fire Department. He was also an auctioneer and merchant, and had formed a partnership with Sol Star in the hardware business.

Despite all that, the greatest achievement of Bullock's first years in the American West was the 1872 Yellowstone Act that created Yellowstone National Park, a gift held in trust for every American, and every visitor to America, to enjoy. Having explored the region on horseback, the conservationist in him made him realize that this unique area needed to be set aside. His resolution called for the preservation of the area, closing it to settlement. His passion was matched by his eloquence and Congress adopted his resolution—though in fairness photographer William H. Jackson shares some of the credit: his 1871 photographs of Yellowstone's natural wonders impressed many in Washington.

The Yellowstone Act was landmark legislation. It was the first time any government had set aside land (two million acres in northwest Wyoming) as a public "pleasuring-ground" and to "preserve their natural beauties." It set a precedent followed by other nations later. The "kid from Canada" literally changed the world.

(Bullock logged an interesting journal entry while exploring Yellowstone: "Numerous hot hell holes, all smelling of sulfur . . . Will recommend this country for religious revivals when I get back. Hell is sure close to the surface here." Those same sulfurous "hellholes" may have inspired an ingenious plan years later when he was sheriff of Deadwood.)

Seth Bullock married his childhood sweetheart, Martha Eccles, from Michigan, in Salt Lake City in 1874. (Neither the Adams Museum archives nor Lynn Bunn's research supports the notion that Bullock married his brother's widow, as portrayed on HBO's *Deadwood*; however, Bullock's chivalry toward his sister-in-law is still accepted Deadwood oral tradition). He could have settled into the sedentary life of a successful businessman in Helena, but there was a gold boom in the nearby Black Hills, and the same sense of adventure that drove him to explore new regions and serve as a peace officer now called him to Deadwood. He sent Martha and their infant daughter back to the safety of Michigan. Then "Bullock and Star loaded wagons with Dutch ovens, fry pans, chamber pots, dynamite, axes, rope, picks and shovels and headed for Deadwood."

"THE NEW-TIME PROPHET"

Con Stapleton, the man appointed sheriff before Bullock in HBO's *Deadwood*, may be based on Isaac "Ike" Brown. According to the Deadwood Underground website, Brown, a "hothead" saloon owner and grocer, was briefly appointed sheriff to guard Jack McCall and protect Judge W. L. Kuykendall during the miner's trial of McCall.

But this was only ad hoc. Seth Bullock was the first real star-packer in Deadwood Gulch. And Sheriff Bullock accomplished exactly the same thing in Deadwood that Wild Bill Hickok had in Abilene and Hays City or Wyatt Earp had in Dodge: He tamed and cleaned up a wild town. He didn't do it with guns blazing, however, but through "strength of character and creativity." He did something few of the gunfighting lawmen did: he became a stabilizing force who helped a struggling pioneer settlement evolve into a flourishing permanent township.

The murder of Wild Bill, only one day after Seth Bullock and Sol Star arrived in Deadwood, did not precipitate an immediate clamor for law and order in the region. It was several months before Bullock was appointed sheriff by the miners, an appointment made official in the spring of 1877 by the territorial governor.

In the meantime, the Indian threat never materialized, Argonauts continued to flood in, and Bullock and Star were rolling in money. Just as depicted in episode 1 of the HBO series, their very first night in Deadwood had Seth putting his auctioneering talents to good use by selling off every chamber pot they had in stock. Within that first year, the ambitious partners had erected a store and office building on Main Street.

Perhaps it was his sound business sense that made Seth Bullock such an effective sheriff. That and his intimidating appearance. (Timothy Olyphant makes a great Bullock, but the actor's striking good looks soften the hard edges of the real man). "Tall and erect, with steely gray eyes peering from beneath bushy eyebrows," *Deadwood Magazine* describes him, "Sheriff Bullock had an imposing appearance that commanded instant respect. 'He could outstare a mad cobra or a rogue elephant,' his grandson said."

Despite that steely gray stare, Bullock did not fashion himself on the gunfighter-lawman image of Hickok, Earp, or Bat Masterson. He relied on courage, intelligence, creative thinking, and some good men backing him up. In almost no time at all, with "little fanfare or gunsmoke," Deadwood joined other law-and-order towns.

Seth Bullock's style of law enforcement was put to the test in November 1877. A tense standoff gripped Deadwood, the Cavalry was called in, and a shoot-out seemed all but certain. A group of about thirty miners had taken over a mine outside the town in a dispute over wages. In those days, discipline was brutal and bloody resolutions to such disputes were common.

But Bullock's instincts favored a minimum of violence. Perhaps recalling his trip to Yellowstone years earlier, and those sulfur-belching hellholes, Sheriff Bullock lowered burning sulfur into the mine and flushed out the miners, who "meekly surrendered."

Later, Bullock would be appointed a deputy U.S. marshal while keeping his other irons in many fires. He raised cattle and horses near present-day Belle Fourche, which he founded, and which went on to become the major livestock-shipping hub in the nation. Politics, mining, such conservation projects as securing the Black Hills' first federal fish hatchery and promoting the Black Hills in general, kept him busy. He also planted the first alfalfa fields in South Dakota, where today it remains an important crop.

In 1884, Deputy Marshal Bullock stopped three suspicious-looking characters out on the range. One of them was Deputy Sheriff Theodore Roosevelt, hot on the trail of a horse thief. The two men, cut from the same frontier cloth, hit it off instantly and remained close friends for life. At Teddy's 1905 presidential inauguration, Bullock led fifty mounted and rowdy cowboys, including silver screen cowboy star Tom Mix, in the inaugural parade.

Being so well rounded and diverse in his interests, Bullock understood the larger picture as few men could. Dime novelists and pop historians alike have a vested interest in scalpings and gunfights. But Bullock understood that it wasn't just Sam Colt's .45 that had tamed the West. It was also barbed wire, the steel plow, and the portable windmill.

Poet Joaquin Miller wrote of "the land from out whose awful depths" shall rise "the new-time prophets." The gunfighter era lasted barely twenty years (circa 1865-85). Long after most of the famous and infamous gunfighters were "dead as a can of corned beef," visionary Bullock was still leading the

Black Hills region into its future.

"Kindly, persistent, firm, full of humor, yet conscious of a vision," the Roosevelt Memorial Association aptly described Seth Bullock in a proclamation. "A frontiersman worthy to walk with the most resourceful and the most courageous and straight American."

POSTSCRIPT: THE EYE THAT NEVER SLEEPS

It's true that Seth Bullock was the first sheriff in Deadwood. But, in a bad scrape, there was another type of policeman available on the western frontier: the operatives of Pinkerton's National Detective Agency, founded by Scottish immigrant Allan Pinkerton in 1850 and still operating today as Pinkerton, Inc.

The botched raid on the James farm in Missouri, mentioned in chapter 4, was not typical of the Pinkerton men. Like the Royal Canadian Mounties, they had a reputation for always getting their man—including out west. A few of the more famous outlaws they locked or helped lock up include Jesse James, Cole Younger, Butch Cassidy and the Sundance

Kid (they didn't capture them but hounded them out of hiding in South America), and the Burrow Gang.

Which explains why Swearengen, in episode three of *Deadwood*, takes it deadly seriously when city slicker Brom Garret threatens to bring the Pinkerton Agency into their dispute over a gold claim. Pinkerton's methods, based on extensive criminal files and infiltration of gangs, were state-of-the-art in their day, giving rise to the modern Secret Service and the FBI's most wanted list. Pinkerton's famous logo (a wide-open eye over the motto "We Never Sleep") once struck fear into many a hard heart.

Ironically, Pinkerton, one of America's premier crime fighters, was himself a fugitive from the law. Branded a political radical in the United Kingdom, he fled Scotland just ahead of the soldiers sent to arrest him. But his father had been a police sergeant (who was killed during a riot) and Pinkerton showed a talent for solving crimes, as a citizen volunteer, helping the Cook County, Illinois, sheriff crack a counterfeiting ring.

As an investigator for Cook County, Pinkerton set a record for burglary and murder arrests. But the money couldn't feed his family, and he opened his own agency at 151 Fifth Avenue in Chicago.

In 1850, the "detective" was still an odd concept to many, and Margaret Pinkerton Fitchett, Pinkerton's granddaughter, noted "it was years before the Pinkerton Agency could be properly described as an established 'success.'" But the railroads, fearful of saboteurs and mail thieves, liked Pinkerton's results, and were important in the agency's eventual expansion across the country.

In 1861, Pinkerton agents uncovered a plot to assassinate Abraham Lincoln in Baltimore. This heads-up work so impressed Union general George McClellan that he asked Pinkerton to become his personal wartime spy. The network of agents (including America's first woman detective, Kate Warne) eventually gave rise to the Secret Service.

Surprisingly, given the widespread fear of them, Pinkerton agents were not recruited for their toughness or shooting ability. Much like Seth Bullock, they were intelligent and resourceful. Pinkerton personally hired every agent, and a high level of literacy was one trait he required. Good, clear reports (which Pinkerton supplied his clients on a daily basis), meticulous criminal records, and infiltrating gangs with well-trained operatives, who were good actors and had high integrity, were the hallmarks of the Pinkerton Agency and its approach.

Pinkerton "ops" (whose ranks have included Dashiell Hammett; The Continental Op is his collection of stories about his Pinkerton days) were never allowed to accept gratuities, relate their adventures in print, or claim a reward even if they earned it. Despite the money it offered, neither would Pinkerton handle divorce cases, reputation being so important. "Above all, no Pinkerton man was allowed to 'frame' evidence to suit a client."

Pinkerton's great-grandson was the last of the Pinkertons to run the company. When he died, it became a corporation, the nation's oldest and largest security services company. Pinkerton reveals his mind and his methods in *Thirty Years a Detective* (1884), a summary of major cases he or his agents cracked between 1852 and 1882.

One of Deadwood's real doctors, Doc F. S. Howe. Courtesy of The Adams Museum & House, Deadwood, South Dakota.

CHAPTER SIX

DEADWOOD'S DOCS AND FRONTIER MEDICINE

Deadwood's Dr. Amos Cochran (Brad Dourif) may be based on one or several of Deadwood's real docs from that early period: Doc Ellis Pierce, who helped Charlie Utter prepare Hickok's body for burial; Doc F. S. Howe, whose duties included caring for prostitutes; or one "Old Doc Babcock," who reportedly worked side by side with Calamity Jane in the smallpox epidemic of 1878. Deadwood also had the distinction, in the 1880s, of having one of the West's first female medicos, Dr. Flora Hayward Stanford.

Secrecy surrounds prostitution, but it's quite likely that the camp's docs competed for lucrative contracts as house doctors for the brothels. Physicians had to scare up work because most people were afraid of doctors and therefore business was often slow. Doc Howe "always took his stomach pump when summoned to the Badlands in the middle of the night" because suicides were so common among soiled doves.

Doc Howe felt compassion for the girls because many of his calls were to treat the results of physical abuse at the hands of customers, employers, or their own husbands and boyfriends. Prostitutes were not covered by the code of chivalry, and many men felt free to let loose on them. No wonder the women turned to opium and alcohol, which only increased their risk for suicide.

It's also reported that Old Doc Babcock joined forces with the gutsy Calamity Jane when the smallpox epidemic swept through the Black Hills and Deadwood. In the HBO version of that event, Doc Cochran has to persuade Calamity to help him; in the actual epidemic, however, she was first in line to volunteer, and, just like the courageous Doc Babcock, "she worked feverishly through the epidemic, nursing people without concern for her own well-being."

Babcock, normally no fan of the vulgar, vituperative Jane, conceded "Oh, she'd swear to beat hell at 'em. But it was a tender kind of cussin'."

Calamity also met and befriended Dr. Flora Hayward Stanford, who was fifty years old when she arrived in a still wild and woolly Deadwood, hoping the climate would improve her ailing daughter's health. With no man to protect her, she purchased a home in Deadwood and hung out her shingle. Her famous patients included Buffalo Bill Cody and Calamity Jane. She became one of the most respected residents of Deadwood—no mean feat for a medical doctor in those days.

A BAG FULL OF NOTHING

Deadwood's Doc Cochran doesn't prescribe laudanum—prescriptions weren't required until 1914, when opium joined a new controlled substances list. Even though he's a pretty good Joe by early Deadwood standards, he virtually pushes it. When Alma Garret (Molly Parker) resists taking laudanum, telling him she wants to break the habit, he flat out advises against that course of action.

But like Deadwood's real docs, Doc Cochran is a good man placed in trying circumstances. In his defense, medicine and medical treatment in the 1870s was a forlorn hope, especially on the frontier. There was no X ray, no ultrasound, no CAT scan, no MRI, few vaccines (and none yet against bacterial infections), no antibiotics (not even penicillin), no aspirin, no insulin, no mammography, no Novocain for dental surgery, no sterilization of equipment, no safe blood transfusion because blood types weren't known, and no preventative medicine.

Alcoholism, widespread in the 1800s, wasn't even seen as a disease, especially since many doctors were tipplers themselves, as well as users of tobacco. Antiseptics were scoffed at, along with Pasteur's weird notions about tiny, invisible microbes causing "bacterial infections." The FDA didn't exist, and not until the 1914 Harrison Narcotic Act was there any regulation of such widely sold drugs as opium and morphine.

Also missing from the medical lexicon in Deadwood days were the notions of "a balanced diet" and "saturated fats," nor had "hormones" entered the picture by name. The immune system, the nervous system, and the lymphatic system weren't understood yet. Oncology, the study of cancer, was barely under way, and psychosomatic disorders were not understood beyond hysteria. Stress? Forget it, and drink your laudanum! The real wonder is that anyone survived a visit to the doctor in those days.

Doc Cochran isn't insensitive, just a product of his education and the severely limited options for a frontier doc. When the prostitute Trixie (Paula Malcomson) asks Doc Cochran for some genuine medicine, to help Alma with the pain of opium withdrawal, he's forced to give her an herbal nostrum. But that's not proof of Cochran's ignorance of legitimate medicines—there simply weren't many available.

A typical frontier doc of the 1870s packed a simple medical kit. If he was thirty or older, his bag was likely still stocked with the most common medicine of the first half of the century: calomel, a purgative thought to expel disease-causing poisons. It was useless medicinally, highly toxic, and could destroy teeth and gums. The doc would also have castor oil, nux vomica (name of the tree from whose poisonous seeds strychnine is derived, a dangerous poison used as a "nervous stimulant"), jalap (a cathartic powder), splints, forceps, and a stethoscope. Most likely he also had some of the best-selling patent medicines of the day (more on that later) even though he knew they were useless and sometimes downright harmful.

Treatment options improved only slowly. Even fifty-seven years after the heyday of Deadwood, "there were ten drugs recognized by physicians as useful and potent," recalls Dr. Randolph H. Kampmeier, an emeritus professor of medicine who graduated medical school out west in 1923. "People would make their own diagnosis and take their own medicines."

All of Deadwood's early docs faced more than a dearth of effective medicines. They were products of the day's science, which taught some of the most insupportable, even dangerous, theories imaginable while rejecting sound, empirically proven notions, such as washing hands before surgery, with a vengeance. In fact, the father of nineteenth-century medical practice, Dr. Benjamin Rush, is today "remembered as the man responsible for more blood loss than any general in U.S. history."

NOXIOUS MIASMA

Deadwood's first docs may have begun to reject some of Benjamin Rush's more bizarre treatment methods because, mercifully, his influence began to wane by the 1870s (as the body count rose and patients rebelled). But a few of his notions about the cause of diseases persisted for most of the century despite the overwhelming evidence from Pasteur, Lister, and others that he was wrong.

Backed by the prestige of the country's first medical institute, associated with the University of Pennsylvania at the start of the nineteenth century, Rush persuaded thousands of physicians and students to adopt his system of "heroic" medicine, and they in turn indoctrinated generations to come. The

"Hippocrates of American medicine," as his devotees dubbed him, did have enlightened views about the mentally ill, to his credit. But sadly for the millions who would suffer and die because of his treatments, he also believed that many contagious diseases, such as the terrible killer yellow fever, were caused by "noxious miasmas," or pockets of poisoned atmosphere.

For decades, because of Rush's widely disseminated ideas, cities like New Orleans fought the plague with artillery cannons aimed into the sky to "blast apart the miasma." But the miasma was not such a foolish theory in the pre-microbial world. They knew about epidemics, of course, and even learned that rodents and birds could spread diseases. But somehow the germ theory gained slow acceptance in America despite the proof of "animalcules" (microbes) as early as 1677. The atmosphere was the focus of evil, in Rush's view, not invisible pathogens.

What eventually made Benjamin Rush controversial was his heroic medicine and its reliance on bleeding, regurgitating, purging, and sweating treatments to "relieve nervous constriction of blood vessels." At its most heroic, Rush's system had the poor, suffering patient purging from every orifice at once. No wonder doctors then were so widely distrusted.

Everybody knew of somebody who'd been bled or purged to death, and a natural resentment at these elitist schoolmen took hold as the country became more democratic in its outlook, less awed by authority. Doctors were acceptable, most felt, for setting bones, digging out bullets, or removing decayed teeth (many frontier docs doubled as dentists). But their horrible record at diagnosis often made surgeries or treatment of acute illnesses more risky than no treatment at all.

Nothing from this period is more astounding, more needlessly wasteful of human life, than the medical profession's arrogant rejection of simple sterilization procedures for decades after they had been dramatically proven to save lives. Many surgeries, even the most simple, resulted in deaths due to postoperative infection. Even into the 1880s, surgeons operated wearing street clothing and without washing their hands or sterilizing their instruments.

It was a direct failure of medical education as well as more proof of the contempt many early physicians showed toward any critics of their blind dogma. The existence of microbes was proven to the Royal Society of London in 1677. In 1847, Hungarian physician Ignaz Phillip Semmelweis asserted that women were dying of childbed fever because of infectious decayed matter transmitted by doctors who'd been in contact with ill patients and cadavers. He began sterilization procedures with chlorine solution, and the death rate decreased dramatically.

Semmelweis's findings were published but as stated above, ignored for decades. As was Pasteur, who proved the dangerous nature of microbes and also proved that "pasteurization" (sterilization by heat) was a powerful weapon against microscopic pathogens. He, too, was virtually ignored by American medicos, who were still busy bleeding, purging, and lethally infecting terrified patients.

In the Civil War, for every soldier killed in battle two more died of infectious diseases (560,000 on the Union side alone). The newly created U.S. Sanitary Commission, directed by Frederick Law Olmstead, began "preaching the virtues of clean water, good food, and fresh air" to control epidemics. Yet, despite implementing changes Olmstead recommended, the Army ignored "antiseptic surgery," just as it ignored anesthesia.

In 1867, British surgeon Joseph Lister published an article on the use of carbolic acid as an antiseptic in wound treatment. Eventually, his findings would revolutionize surgery by making it much more survivable, but at first he, too, was widely discredited and ignored. Unenlightened resistance greeted, and fought, every major advance in medicine, including anesthesia

"The abolishment of pain in surgery is a chimera," scoffed Dr. Alfred Velpeau, a professor of medicine in Paris, only six years before the first demonstration of etherized anesthesia. "It is absurd to go on seeking it. Knife and pain are two words in surgery that must forever be associated in the consciousness of the patient."

Some resistance to change is inevitable, but it is staggering how long the germ theory went ignored, especially out west. Much of the blame falls squarely on medical education itself. Deadwood's first docs, Babcock, Ellis and Howe, were most likely educated by proprietary (that is, private and for profit) medical schools and the apprentice system. Only near the end of the nineteenth century would medical schools emphasize laboratory work and clinical practice. Deadwood's first docs received mostly theoretical lectures about the human body with little hands-on backup.

Doc Cochran's apparent lack of empathy toward Alma Garret's addiction reflects a man who saw himself as a profiteering tradesman more than a compassionate professional. After all, when men like Cochran went to medical school there were likely no entrance requirements. All students (some illiterate) purchased tickets to hear lectures. The schools were a business, owned by the doctors who lectured there, and high standards of admission would have killed the cash cow.

In fairness, many schools were also hindered by laws that were too often shaped by religious views. Dissection of human corpses is fundamental to truly learning human anatomy, yet well into the century many states prohibited human dissection. Students had to provide their own bodies or pay body snatchers hired by some schools to rob fresh graves.

THE PEOPLE'S CHOICE: DR. QUACK

Not surprisingly, most ailing citizens in nineteenth-century America feared doctors and avoided them like the plague. Good Health magazine began publishing in 1866, an early sign that more Americans were interested in prevention as an alternative to often risky medical treatment.

Unfortunately, what quickly rose to fill the healthcare vacuum was "The Great American Fraud," as muckraking journalist Samuel Hopkins Adams called the powerful and wealthy ($75 million annually at its peak) patent medicine industry.

A guaranteed cure-all? Patent medicine bottle from a Deadwood pharmacy. Courtesy of The Adams Museum & House, Deadwood, South Dakota.

Patent medicines were useless nostrums often laced with alcohol (Lydia E. Pinkham's Vegetable Compound, twenty percent alcohol and the most successful patent medicine of all time), opium (Tott's Teething Cordial, "Satisfies the Baby, pleases the Mother, gives rest to both"), and cocaine (Casseebeer's Coca-Calisaya, "Each tablespoon represents about one gramme of the best Peruvian Coca Leaves"). Wildly hyped as cure-alls, they were the nation's first real mass-market advertising success.

However, "patent medicine" was a misnomer. Usually, only the shape of the bottle or the design of promotional material was patented. A patent on the actual formula would have revealed the drug and alcohol content—and many of patent medicines' most loyal customers were temperance ladies.

Each medicine made the grandiose claim it was the key to total health and happiness. They claimed to cure diseases we still haven't cured today: Tubercolozine ("The New Remedy for Consumption"), Dr. Lindley's Epilepsy Remedy ("For Epilepsy, Fits, Spasms, Convulsions and St. Vitus Dance"), Warner's Safe Diabetes Remedy, Mixer's Cancer and Scrofula Syrup ("Cures Cancer, Tumors, Abscesses, Ulcers, Fever Sores, Goiter, Catarrh, Scald Head, Piles, Rheumatism and ALL BLOOD DISEASES").

Not everyone believed these miracle claims, of course. After all, the more popular nostrums were often sold by the local doctor. But all forms of quackery were widespread as millions of desperate Americans tried to find some relief for health problems and the related emotional stress. Mesmerism ("animal magnetism" causes illness), electropathy ("Magical properties of electricity will cure you!"), hydropathy ("Wash and be healed!"), and spiritualism were just some of the movements inspired, in part, by the abysmal state of nineteenth-century medicine.

The phenomenal success of the junk medicine business was also due to the newspapers (more than four thousand by the time of the Civil War) in which these nostrums were heavily advertised, often with long testimonials. But the citizens of Deadwood, and most frontier towns, were also visited by medicine shows. These were traveling variety shows whose entertainers (singers, acrobats, magicians, trick shooters) were merely lures to draw a crowd. Between acts, a "doctor" made sales pitches for the company line.

The 1906 Pure Food and Drug Act (requiring full disclosure of contents on labels) and the 1914

Harrison Narcotic Act killed much of the patent medicine business. But so great was its influence that "the name that launched a million bottles" (Lydia E. Pinkham's Vegetable Compound) is owned by Cooper Laboratories and still on the market today — presumably, with a new formula.

According to legend, Marshall Wyatt Earp's visit to Deadwood did not sit well with Sheriff Bullock. (Denver Public Library, Western History Collection, Z-246).

CHAPTER SEVEN

GUNFIGHTERS, GAMBLERS, AND GONERS: DEADWOOD'S FAMOUS VISITORS

A peregrine falcon soars high on the wind's current; frothing streams disappear as they plunge underground. Clouds tend to gather quickly over the isolated peaks here, and the danger of lightning is constant even on sunny days. The Cheyenne, cousins and battle allies of the Lakota, once painted their arrows blue to symbolize a sacred lake in these Black Hills. They called the hills simply Wakan Tanka, the "Great Mystery."

Some places have a natural ability to lure visitors and instill a sense of wonder. The Black Hills and Deadwood have drawn the famous and the infamous, gamblers, writers, artists, presidents, athletes, movie stars. According to the Historic Deadwood Web site, just some of those visitors include the real "Deadwood Dick," Sitting Bull, Wild Bill Hickok, Buffalo Bill Cody, Crazy Horse, Sam Bass, Babe Ruth, Wyatt Earp, Gutzon Borglum (starting work on Mt. Rushmore in 1927), William Jennings Bryan, Calamity Jane, the Sundance Kid, Calvin Coolidge, Mark Twain, George Armstrong Custer, Bat Masterson, Big Foot (the Lakota, not the hirsute creature), Poker Alice, Black Elk, Aunt Sally, and Teddy Roosevelt.

Books have been written about all of them, and most have been featured in movies. What follows are brief profiles of eight of these illustrious visitors whose names will be forever associated with Deadwood and the Black Hills.

NAT LOVE (THE REAL "DEADWOOD DICK")

By the thousands, black cowboys followed the trails west after the Civil War (eventually, one of every four cowboys was black). Frontier life was hard for them. Killers like avowed racists John Wesley Hardin and Bill Longley, both Texans, "had the anti-Negro complex" and murdered unarmed blacks in cold blood. But it was often even harder back in the postwar South, where Reconstruction caused resentment and triggered night riders. At least out west, a competent black cowboy could earn some grudging respect from other cowboys.

Nat Love, born a slave in Tennessee in 1854, was "poor as a hind-tit calf" when he came west to wide-open Dodge City and became a top hand, a damn good cowboy. He hazed cattle up the famous Chisolm Trail. In 1876 he published his colorful autobiography The Life and Adventures of Nat Love, (Better Known in the Cattle Country as "Deadwood Dick.")

In his book, Love claimed to have entered a rodeo in Deadwood, where one of his prizes was the honorary title Deadwood Dick. One year after Love's book came out, Ned Buntline published his first of many novels about "Deadwood Dick, the Black Rider of the Black Hills." Buntline ("Colonel" Edward Zane Carroll Judson) never resolved the issue of the true person, if any, behind Deadwood Dick, and at least five men claimed they inspired the character.

But even if the name was just coincidence,

Deadwood historians agree, Nat Love stands for all time as the only real Deadwood Dick.

BUFFALO BILL CODY, AMERICA'S SHOWMAN

Among those who showed up in Deadwood in the aftermath of J. B. Hickok's death was his longtime friend and admirer, William Frederick "Buffalo Bill" Cody, a hunter, Indian fighter, and U.S. Army scout turned flamboyant showman. His "Buffalo Bill's Wild West and Congress of Rough Riders of the World" show would soon become the greatest spectacle of its day.

Cody was only twelve years old when he worked for a wagon train bound for Laramie, thirteen when he participated in the Colorado gold rush, fifteen when he rode for the Pony Express. He was one of only four civilian scouts to win the Congressional Medal of Honor for valor during the Indian Wars. But he never took Indian fighting personally. In fact, it wasn't all that long after Little Bighorn before he "hired some of the same Indians who had fought Custer" to start killing old Iron Butt over and over again as part of Cody's Wild West Show.

Buffalo Bill's show opened in Omaha in 1883 and ran for thirty years, making him wealthy and "the most famous American in the world." Cody didn't want actors, recruiting real Indians and real cow-boys and cow-girls (the hyphen was used then, the terms were so new) at a time when most found the cowboy to be a low and common creature. By the end of the century, though, Cody's show had changed all that. His shows, which included bronco riding and roping, were the forerunner to rodeos. The Wild West Show was a smash hit in England at Queen Victoria's Golden Jubilee in 1887 and was even credited with improving British and American relations.

Whooping Indians, silver-trimmed saddles, fringed buckskins, blazing six-shooters—never mind the simplistic melodrama of Buffalo Bill's show, it defined the Wild West for the rest of the world. And he was always the star, not Sitting Bull or the other celebrities he hired, not even trick shooter Annie Oakley, whom he called "Little Sure Shot." His golden curls, his fancy hats, his ornately embroidered jackets and bright satin sashes—like Hickok, he was a bit of a dandy, and he was often drunk before noon. But Buffalo Bill Cody was a first-rate frontiersman who earned his legend by his deeds.

CRAZY HORSE, PRIDE OF THE LAKOTA

There were many great Lakota battle leaders, including Sitting Bull, Red Cloud, and Gall. But Crazy Horse (Tashunca-uitco) possessed something else besides skill in battle: "a fierce determination to preserve his people's way of life."

Beginning in his teen years, Crazy Horse fought in many battles, especially against the Crows, the Shoshones, and the U.S. Army. Eight days before the Battle of the Little Bighorn, Crazy Horse led the brilliant Lakota victory at the Battle of the Rosebud River, routing Civil War veteran General George Crook and eleven hundred troops. Then "Crazy Horse was at the head of the attack which pinned and later wiped out Custer on the ridge of the famous Last Stand."

Crazy Horse didn't "visit" the Black Hills; by law, his people owned them, and he went hunting in Deadwood Gulch before the first whites ever set camp.

Later, when the Lakota were herded off to reservations, a white man mocked him by saying "Where are your lands now?" Crazy Horse replied, "My lands are where my dead lie buried."

Crazy Horse is a hero to the Lakota because he never sold out to the white man. Sitting Bull ended up in Buffalo Bill's Wild West Show, where he used to sell his autograph (an X) for a dollar and pose for photographs (although it's said he gave the money to poor children). Crazy Horse, in contrast, though famous among whites, refused to be photographed.

"My friend," he once asked a photographer, "why should you wish to shorten my life by taking from me my shadow?"

SAM BASS AND THE "BLACK HILLS BANDITS"

His fame has diminished somewhat, but Sam Bass's legend once extended even to stodgy old Great Britain, where a wax version of him was featured at Madame Tussaud's Waxworks in London. The very name of Sam Bass once struck terror even into the hearts of the stalwart Texas Rangers, who feared that his folk hero status meant he had a "criminal army" waiting to rise up at any time.

Also known as "Texas' Beloved Bandit" and "Robin Hood on a Fast Horse," Sam Bass is the subject of movies (such as Sam Bass and Calamity Jane), songs ("The Ballad of Sam Bass," a cowboy favorite), and more than two hundred books. Many of them contradictory because legend and lore have overtaken the facts about Sam Bass.

Some who have studied this "inept" man of "shallow conscience" are baffled by his astounding folk hero status. He murdered good men in cold blood, and that's not Robin Hood's style.

Bass and his partner Joel Collins showed up in Deadwood in 1876 with $8,000 burning a hole in their pockets. They owed the money to some Texas cattlemen whose beef they drove to market, but they liked the boom times in Deadwood. The Robin Hood version says they lost their money prospecting in the Black Hills, but it seems more likely they lost "the swag" to sharper minds at the gambling tables or perhaps while playing craps at the Bella Union.

Broke, they gave the freighting business a try but failed. Bass and Collins next formed the gang that became the "Black Hills Bandits."

There was perhaps as much bungling as banditry. Sam and Joel "masterminded" seven stagecoach heists in a row without a decent take. Witnesses to their later train robberies in Texas, too, called them amateurish, noting that the gang twice "missed large stashes of money."

But Sam Bass was exceptional at escape and avoidance, a benefit of his youth spent freighting and learning the roads. It took the four-month "Bass War" to capture this storied outlaw, and the Texas Ranger who probably shot him denied it to his grave, fearing someone in the (nonexistent) Bass Army would get him.

AN ICON WINTERS IN DEADWOOD: WYATT EARP

Wyatt Earp and his brother Morgan (who was shot in the back six years later in Tombstone) arrived in Deadwood only a few weeks after Wild Bill was murdered. But all the claims were taken by then, just as Bat Masterson had warned the Earps. Rather than turn to gambling, at which he was adept, Wyatt put brain and muscle into a sure-fire business: hauling winter stove wood to residents of the area.

One night a gambler, notes *Deadwood Magazine*, anxious to keep a game going all night, paid Wyatt's premium rate, "one hundred dollars a cord and ten dollars for my helper—the thermometer was at forty below zero that night and there was a forty-mile northwest wind howling." Hard, cold work, but by spring Wyatt left Deadwood, riding shotgun on $200,000 in gold, with a profit of about five thousand dollars.

Wyatt Berry Stapp Earp, who was lanky and ruggedly handsome, witnessed gun battles in Deadwood but avoided trouble himself while there. He had already made a name for himself as a lawman in Wichita and Dodge, where sensation-hungry newspaper hacks were feeding his exploits to the Associated Press and its system of shared telegraphic dispatches. Earp, like Hickok, Cody, and other crack shots, was a national celebrity.

Seth Bullock's grandson, Ken Kellar, reports that

at some point during Wyatt Earp's visit, Earp and Bullock had a "showdown" of sorts. Perhaps Earp was eyeing Sheriff Bullock's job, but if so, Bullock convinced him that his services weren't required. Marshall Earp took his advice and left town.

It wasn't until he arrived in Tombstone, Cochise County, Arizona Territory, that Wyatt Earp etched his name deep. Sided by the legendary John Henry "Doc" Holliday and Wyatt's brothers Virgil and Morgan, Earp faced down that proverbial hail of lead in the most famous Western gunfight of them all, the "shootout at the OK Corral."

That notorious 1881 "cartridge session" was the result of an escalating feud between the Clanton outlaws and the Earps. Sources repeatedly allude to the "sixty-second gun battle," but former Wyatt Earp deputy A. M. King insisted, in 1959, "The battle only lasted thirty seconds according to my friend Wyatt Earp." That's hearsay, not proof, but thirty seconds also fits the total rounds fired ("over thirty," according to eyewitness R. F. Coleman as reported in the Tombstone Epitaph; the figure accepted today is thirty-one).

To this day it's not really clear to everyone who the "heroes" were, if any. Wyatt, like many lawmen of that day, often had some side ventures of a shady nature.

"A PLUMB GOOD SORT": THEODORE ROOSEVELT

"There must be the keenest sense of duty," Theodore Roosevelt wrote in the foreword to his 1913 autobiography, "and with it must go the joy of living." Roosevelt (widely known as "Teddy" and "T.R.") did indeed visit Deadwood often, including a visit to the "Days of '76" parade after he was president. But they were the visits of a man returning to his old home ranges and friends, to the country that shaped him for life.

In 1883, T. R. was an asthmatic young Harvard alum who left his New York home "to find solace and good health" on a Dakota cattle ranch. He described the Far West of that day as "a land of scattered ranches, of herds of long-horned cattle, and of reckless riders who unmoved looked in the eyes of life or death."

Eventually, he started his own ranch near present-day Medora, North Dakota (the Elkhorn brand marked his cattle). Roosevelt redefined himself in the West. The rugged, short-grass country, with its life of "manly vigor," allowed him to develop key personality traits that raised eyebrows in the urbanized, "civilized" East. Until the end of his days, he insisted that his years in the Dakota country were "the most important educational asset of all my life."

No question, though, that Teddy got off to a shaky start in the cowboy arts. On one of his first cattle drives he attempted to "haze" the beeves with the shout, "Hasten forward quickly there!" The cowboys cracked up.

But they came to admire this bespectacled greenhorn who "had more guts than a smokehouse." In fact, the first best-selling cowboy novel (Owen Wister's The Virginian, 1902) was dedicated to T.R.

POKER ALICE

The South Dakota State Historical Society Web site offers this note for the years 1928: "Gov. Bulow pardons Poker Alice, 78, after she is convicted on a bootlegging charge. Gov. Bulow was said to be reluctant to send a white-haired old lady to prison."

Of course the governor was reluctant: by 1928, gambler, bootlegger, and madam "Poker Alice" Ivers was a full-blown Black Hills and Deadwood legend. The cigar; the pretty but remarkably impersonal face; the ".38 on a .45 frame" she always carried—these features, and her incredible luck at poker (she made up to $6,000 a night in her prime, surpassing the entire take of the Gem) made Poker Alice a familiar face at "serious" games.

Born in England, the daughter of a schoolmaster, and educated in a female seminary, Alice Ivers turned to gambling after her first husband, Frank Duffield, was killed in a dynamite explosion. She met her next husband, card dealer Warren G. Tubbs, while gambling in Deadwood. As one version has it: "One night a drunken miner pulled a knife on him [Tubbs]. Alice deftly palmed her .38 and pumped a slug into the miner's arm, triggering a romance between Tubbs and herself."

Tubbs died during a blizzard, and Alice hauled his frozen corpse in a sled for nearly fifty miles to Sturgis, where she hocked her wedding ring to cover his burial. Her last years were often desperate as her beauty was gone and the wide-open card games grew scarce. She took to bootlegging and running a whorehouse in Sturgis. And she married briefly a third time, to George Huckert.

But harsh realities can't quash legends. Poker Alice is still represented in Deadwood's "Days of '76" parade, where she remains the queen of female gamblers.

INTERNATIONAL MAN OF MYSTERY:
THE SUNDANCE KID

A Pinkerton recorded this description of the Sundance Kid (Harry Alonzo Longabaugh): "32—5 ft 10. 175—Med. Comp. Firm expression in face, German descent Combs his hair Pompadour, it will not lay smooth."

It cost Longabaugh eighteen months in the Sundance, Wyoming, jail (for horse theft) to earn the moniker Sundance Kid for life. Later, captured after a shootout with the "law dogs" in Montana in 1897, Sundance was taken to the Lawrence County jail in

Deadwood and held for the robbery of a Belle Fourche, South Dakota, bank. But after several weeks of Deadwood's hospitality he escaped, and as a member of the infamous Wild Bunch became one of the West's most successful bank and train robbers.

Most fans of Western lore, however, associate Sundance with his friend and partner, Robert LeRoy Parker, aka Butch Cassidy. And two "factions" have emerged: Those who believe Sundance and Butch were killed in San Vicente, Bolivia, on November 6, 1908, and those who believe they cleverly faked their own deaths, had plastic surgery, and returned to the American West, living under new identities.

It's not likely to ever be resolved, but there's less evidence for the fake deaths version than the died in Bolivia take. On the other hand, the PBS science program NOVA exhumed the remains in the Bolivian grave in 1991, "but DNA tests ruled out Butch and Sundance."

CHAPTER EIGHT

"STRAIGHT AND COURAGEOUS": A FEW OF DEADWOOD'S REAL HEROES

David Lavender opined, regarding the "imported professional gunmen" such as Wyatt Earp and Wild Bill Hickok: "The names are more familiar than those of the . . . leading bankers and cattle brokers, to say nothing of the first ministers and schoolteachers."

Teddy Roosevelt and others blamed this romanticizing of criminals on the medieval Robin Hood legend. Perhaps the criminal-romanticizing excesses of the French Revolution also shaped the frontier mythos. By filtering the history of the American West through the simplistic lens of folktales, we get a distorted view of these so-called heroes.

However, the fact that cold-blooded, sometimes

even psychotic killers could be called Robin Hood is also a sad reflection on the nineteenth-century abuses by some people in power, especially the railroad tycoons. Their forced displacement of settlers, horrible safety record, deliberate lies about life on the Plains, refusal (at first) to protect passengers on trains—these and other abuses helped to create the Robin Hood as avenger mind-set.

Wild Bill Hickok was not a criminal, as opposed to Jesse James, Sam Bass, the Sundance Kid and others. He spent barely three weeks in camp, and yet his legend is forever entwined into Deadwood's history. The following are among hundreds of actual "Black Hillers" who hung on through adversity and helped ensure that a lawless gold-strike camp would make the transition to a thriving community.

"HE DIED IN THE HARNESS": PREACHER SMITH

Methodist reverend Henry Weston Smith, known to generations of Black Hills residents simply as "Preacher Smith," was a virtual stranger when he arrived in Deadwood in 1876, the Gulch's first

Henry Winston Smith, known to Deadwood residents as Preacher Smith. Courtesy of The Adams Museum & House, Deadwood, South Dakota.

itinerant clergyman. Only after his mysterious murder did folks begin to realize what manner of man had come among them.

Deadwood's Reverend H. W. Smith (Ray McKinnan) appears to be in his 30s; the real Preacher Smith was nearly 50 when he arrived in Deadwood. And although Deadwood has him officiating at Wild Bill's funeral (he was in town when Hickok was killed), in reality no clergyman officiated. Like Wild Bill, his friends had little use for clergy.

On August 20, only eighteen days after Hickok was laid to rest, Preacher Smith left a note promising to return by two o'clock, then left on foot to preach a sermon in Camp Crook (also called "Crook City," a ghost town today) eight miles from Deadwood. He never returned. Later his dead body, shot in the chest, was found along the trail.

The murderer was never identified or caught, and the crime is one of the hills' great unsolved mysteries, along with the murder of a beautiful Chinese woman called "Yellow Doll." Seth Bullock, in a letter to one of Smith's friends, blamed Smith's murder on Indians, but if there was any proof it hasn't survived. Some think that the same criminal faction in Deadwood who had Hickok killed also "did for" the Rev. Both Hickok and Smith had a dangerous tendency toward moral uprightness. In Deadwood, that was bad for business.

Locals learned a few things about Smith after his death. This humble, pious man had known both suffering and prosperity. His wife and infant son died only a year after marriage. During the Civil War, he served in the Massachusetts 52nd Infantry. After the war, he was licensed as a physician before answering his calling to the ministry.

Postscript: August 1876 was a dangerous month in the Black Hills. On the day Preacher Smith was murdered, Charles Mason was also killed near Crook City. He was buried along with Preacher Smith in the same grave. And the evening before, pony mail carrier Charles "Red" Nolin was bringing mail to Deadwood when he was ambushed, killed, and scalped.

MAYOR SOL STAR

Deadwood's Sol Star (played by John Hawkes) is a

loosely accurate physical and character match for his real-life counterpart. "An apostle of the private mercenary interest as an organizing principle of behavior," he's described in the show's cast of characters, "Sol Star is pure entrepreneur."

But in real life he wasn't quite that one-dimensional. Consider this excerpt from the September 1881 headlines: "Sol Star was removed from office as Postmaster of Deadwood on the charge of 'complicity with star route carrier (contractor) in arranging arbitrary arrival of mails.' Star was probably not guilty, but was a victim of a sinister plot."

Probably so, because a few years later Sol Star was elected mayor. An immigrant from Bavaria, he was certainly a skilled businessman and an important merchant in Deadwood and regionally. But he was also a public servant, and his Jewish heritage emphasized community building. Star was one of Deadwood's first councilmen, elected in 1876 when the town voted to incorporate. He held a brief tenure as postmaster before serving as mayor for fourteen years, and as clerk of courts for twenty years once

Lawrence County was established. He also served in the South Dakota State Legislature and as president of the Senate.

Star Bullock Hardware was only part of a far-flung Black Hills business empire. He and Bullock sold the first farm machinery in the area, in 1878, a sign they were already looking beyond the mining boom. They soon had livestock interests in Belle Fourche, as well as other ventures in Sturgis, Spearfish, and Custer. And they joined forces with Harris Franklin (of Franklin Hotel fame) in the Deadwood Flouring Mill Company.

While Star was Mayor of Deadwood, he enjoyed the privilege of being one of only two non-Chinese allowed at ceremonies in the Masonic Lodge in Deadwood's Chinese community. He had worked hard to smooth relations between the two communities, seeing in the Chinese the same strong work ethic he admired in others. In 1899 he also hosted international firebrand-radical populist William Jennings Bryan when he made a stop in Deadwood on his presidential campaign and stayed with Star.

I. C. H. Grabill, Photographer,
DEADWOOD AND STURGIS, DAKOTA TER.

Sol Star served as Deadwood's mayor for fourteen years, in addition to his business partnership with Seth Bullock. Courtesy of The Adams Museum & House, Deadwood, South Dakota.

WILD BILL'S PARD: "COLORADO" CHARLIE UTTER

No wonder Charlie Utter's wagon train, which arrived in Deadwood Gulch in July 1876, is now called historic. Colorado Charlie (played by Dayton Callie) not only had Wild Bill Hickok along but also Calamity Jane, two madams (Madam Dirty Em and Madam Mustachio, though there are alternate spellings), and the town's first batch of sporting girls. They all had just been run out of Fort Laramie.

Charlie Utter was a well-known, well-liked trapper, prospector, packer, and guide. The real Colorado Charlie was probably a bit more assertive and flamboyant than his counterpart on Deadwood; after all, he wore "revolvers mounted in gold, silver and pearl," notes Deadwood Magazine. He once appeared "in Prince Albert coat and top hat, wearing a two-foot watch chain made of gold coins set with diamonds and rubies."

It's not known exactly when he and Wild Bill met, but everyone considered them partners. He was seeing to the affairs of his latest business venture, a Pony Express service, when Jack McCall "hurled Wild

Bill into eternity."

Utter quickly took charge of his pard's body and fate. He published a notice of Wild Bill's death and a funeral announcement, then buried him in a hillside plot he paid for himself. Years later, when the body was relocated to Mt. Moriah Cemetery overlooking Deadwood, Charlie Utter oversaw it. In 1880, amid rumors a New York museum was going to dig Bill up, Charlie returned from Colorado to Deadwood to guard the plot. For years he kept himself fully informed about Wild Bill's grave and any plans for it.

From a graveside tribute left by Charlie: "Pard, we will meet again in the happy hunting ground to part no more. Good-bye, Colorado Charlie, C.H. Utter."

W. E. ADAMS

The period 1878 to 1887 is called the "Great Dakota Boom." With new railroads making settlement much more attractive, "pilgrims" flocked to Dakota. But the railroads weren't as quick to reach the Black Hills (not until the 1890s). In Deadwood's first years especially, that area was still a "hive of free-ranging Indians."

Which scared off railroad crews and made it that much more profitable for those first intrepid merchants into Deadwood Gulch. It was a seller's market.

Among the first waves was gutsy Michigander Will Emery Adams. He knew that hardware and groceries were a booming concern in the 1870s. Especially with the immense freighting difficulties that caused widespread scarcity of goods basic to survival. W. E. Adams immediately saw how eager the Argonauts were to part with their gold dust. But Adams earned his money by hard work and square dealing, not deceit.

Just like Bullock and Star, Adams arrived in Deadwood hauling a load of hardware. With his brother James, he opened the Adams Brothers Banner Grocery in 1877. By 1901, having bounced back from two fires and a flood, he had ventured into wholesale, operating one of the largest businesses in the state. But he also showed the public spirit of Sol Star by serving as mayor of Deadwood for six terms, establishing several parks, and giving the city the Adams Memorial Museum (tapped heavily by Deadwood's writers) as a gift.

Late in Adams' life, tragedy struck—in triplicate. In 1925, when he was 71, his wife, Alice, traveled to California for the birth of their daughter Helen's first child. Alice, ill with cancer, died on June 6, 1925. A grief-stricken Helen "went into labor and died the next day. The baby died soon afterward, and was buried in her mother's arms." In the span of two days, Adams lost his wife, daughter, and granddaughter.

But the old gent's fires weren't banked yet. W. E. began a "scandalous" second marriage (she was Catholic, he Episcopalian) with a twenty-nine-year-old Lead widow, Mary Mastrovich Vicich.

MADAM DORA DUFRAN ("D. DEE")

Deadwood series creator David Milch has mixed real characters from the past with imaginary types. Trixie (played by Paula Malcomson) isn't an actual sporting girl from the old Gem, but she could be based, at least partly, on Madam Dora DuFran (born Amy Bolshow, in England), known affectionately as D. Dee. Like Calamity Jane, both have good hearts and risk danger to help others.

Al Swearengen and his loutish crew made life for a prostitute at the Gem vulgar, demeaning, and dangerous. Dora had a reputation for treating her girls humanely. When Calamity Jane went through some rough sledding at the end of her hard life, Madam DuFran took her in as a cook and laundress for the women in her house of ill repute.

Today, we hardly make note of the worldwide influenza epidemic that struck in 1918, but flu strains were far more dangerous then and by 1920, twenty-two million people had died from it worldwide. It struck America hard, too, and Dora DuFran appointed herself as an unpaid nurse for the duration. Desperate, impoverished patients with no place to go had Dora to turn to. She turned her home into a charity hospital.

D. Dee was also a talented author whose writings include her memoirs and the booklet Low Down on Calamity Jane.

POTATO CREEK JOHNNY

Not all the history makers in Deadwood stood six foot

two, talked tough, and wore a "tie-down gun." Welshman John Perret (a name you probably won't hear Deadwood residents use) was only four foot three, but as "Potato Creek Johnny" he epitomized the grizzled old prospector. He ensured his place in the Black Hills hall of fame when he discovered the largest gold nugget ever known to have been found in the Hills. It weighed 7-3/4 troy ounces.

Johnny's claim on Potato Creek gave him the name everyone knew him by. The nugget itself wasn't all that built Potato Creek Johnny into a legend in his own life. Word spread and tourists began to look him up in his cabin or watch him pan for color. Johnny loved to tell gold camp stories, and visitors were just as eager to hear them. Some people came just to see the famous prospector who made Bret Harte's Roaring Camp tales come to life.

Eventually, Potato Creek Johnny became one of the great tourist draws of the Black Hills. Folks in Deadwood, sniffing another bonanza here, even paid his way to Chicago to promote tourism. As for the "leg-shaped" nugget, W. E. Adams bought it for $250.

The Adams Museum reports that it's stored in their safe-deposit box, but a replica is on display.

OLD DEADWOOD DAYS: SOME NAMES AND PLACES

In the 600 block of Main where the No. 10 Saloon was once located, you'll find the Eagle Bar. And the site of the notorious Gem Theater is now the Mineral Palace. But even today, despite devastating natural and man-made disasters, there are unbroken links to the Deadwood of '76.

Deadwood Gulch pioneer George Ayers, for example, arrived in 1876 and didn't own his own hardware store until 1907. But the firm, "George B. Ayers & Co.," still operates in Deadwood today.

As does the Bullock Hotel at 633 Main Street. The original hotel, built in 1895, "boasted a bathroom on every floor." Since 1990, when it was "restored . . . to its former glory," there have been continuing reports of "paranormal activity" in Bullock Hotel. The popular *Unsolved Mysteries* television series featured the hotel in 1992.

Close in age, and equally historic, is the Franklin

Hotel. Harris Franklin (he changed his name from Finkelstein) was the largest investor in the hotel and said to be Deadwood's richest man. The 1903 Franklin is impressive for its day, with steam radiators, transoms, and claw-footed bathtubs. Literally, every room or suite bears one famous name on the door. The dining room floor creaks just the way it ought to under the weight of all that history. Slots in the lobby, poker in the dining room.

Many more of those original businesses live on in memory or lore: Jake Shoudy's butcher shop, where coward Jack McCall was cornered after murdering Hickok; the Empire Bakery on Sherman Street, where the great fire of '79 started (approximate site of Adams Memorial Museum today); Farnam and Brown's log cabin grocery store on the corner of Main and Gold (this Farnam was a mayor, judge, and solid citizen, unlike the "squirrely" E. B. Farnam [played by William Sanderson] of *Deadwood*). The Montana Saloon was a rough place, and Deadwood, too, had a Lone Star saloon. Pam's Purple Door, the last house of prostitution, closed in 1980, preceded by the Green,

White, and Beige Doors.

At Deadwood's first hotel, Charles Wagner's Grand Central, "Weary travelers paid $1.00 a night for a crudely constructed bunk or just space to spread their own blankets on the floor." Also gone but not forgotten is the old Mansion House hotel on the corner of Wall Street, site of the Fairmont Hotel today.

In the 1870s, John Nye sold tinware and "old man Cohn" sold clothes. John Treber, a German immigrant, became Deadwood's first wholesale liquor dealer. Tom Callahan was friends with Wild Bill and drove the Deadwood stage in 1876. Julius Deetkin was a pharmacist, and twenty-one-year-old Charles Dietrick delivered groceries with a packhorse. A few years later, in Chinatown, Ban Wong ("Benny") managed the OK Café; Wong Kee ("Susie") owned the Bodega Café (best eats in Deadwood); and Fee Lee Wong opened his Wing Tsue Emporium at 596 Main Street selling groceries, imported Chinaware, herbs and novelties.

CHAPTER NINE

DEADWOOD'S CUSSIN' ANGEL: CALAMITY JANE

Many who are tired of the old tintype clichés would like to know the real truth about Calamity Jane. Maybe it's just this simple: she was the American West's greatest bullshit artist ever. And that's saying an impressive mouthful.

She lived an interesting if hard life, and there seems little debate on the matter of her riding and shooting skills—she was "death to the devil." She was also another one of those courageous, compassionate unpaid nurses Deadwood produces in a pinch.

But the truth is, nobody knows much for certain about her—even Calamity's most scholarly biographer admits that right up front. Once the dime novelists and theater agents had latched onto her, Calamity Jane probably realized nobody wanted the truth. They wanted what we call today "the juice" and what people in Jane's era called "tossing in another grizzly."

Almost everything about Calamity Jane, from her real name and birthdate to her true marital status and relationship with Wild Bill Hickok, is in a confused moil because of Jane's "stretchers." The fact that we have only her word she was even married or ever a mother, for example, doesn't mean she wasn't. And that's the genius of her system if that's what it was: give the greenhorns just enough to build their damn hog-stupid legend on but not enough to prove "The White Devil of the Yellowstone" (another flashy name she gave herself) was an out-and-out bullshitter.

It's a testament to Calamity Jane's consummate skills as a spinner of yarns that so many books and articles today recount fabulous tales of her deeds of derring-do, tales almost certainly fabricated from whole cloth "By Herself," to quote the byline from her clumsily ghostwritten pamphlet Life and Adventures of Calamity Jane. Research has shown that the anecdotes in it are apocryphal, but some writers today continue to invoke it as gospel truth.

Date of Birth? She claims 1852 (in Princeton, Missouri), but more reliable sources include a question mark after the date. Evidently, she was feminine enough to vainly shave a few years off her age, and researchers now say no later than 1847 is a more likely year estimate.

Real name? Again, good luck. The Random House Biographical Dictionary lists it as Martha Jane Canary Burke. But "Cannary" with two ns seems the current preference. Jane herself gives her "maiden name" as Martha Cannary—conspicuously failing to reference "Jane" as a middle name. It was probably sneaked in later, to solidify the growing reputation of "Calamity Jane." The "Burke" (sometimes "Burk") was supposedly acquired by marriage, for which no record exists. More moiling confusion. As for the world-famous Calamity Jane moniker, Jane's own little pamphlet spins a cock-and-bull story about how her battlefield heroics led to it. We will probably never know how she got it, but it's worth noting that in some regions of the West "Calamity Jane" was also used

CALAMITY JANE, SCOUT, FREIGHTER AND
FRONTIERSWOMAN

(*From a photograph taken in 1876, found under an old building.*)

interchangeably with "soiled dove" or "sporting girl" as slang for prostitute. So just as a customer was known as a "john," a prostitute was known as a "jane."

Calamity Jane had to have seen plenty of real adventures early on in her life, given that her Ohio-born parents took her and her five younger siblings west to Virginia City, Montana in 1865. It appears she was orphaned by 1868 and on her own from then on.

Jane was nearly six feet tall, "thickset" with masculine features, and she sought work as a teamster and bullwhacker (a "teamster" was a wagon driver, a "bullwhacker" walked beside teams of bulls or oxen and kept them motivated with a "blacksnake," a long, vicious whip). Calamity preferred men's clothing, anyway, and at times she must have passed herself off as a man to get work. Which might explain why an Army colonel who'd hired her as a teamster fired her on the spot when he caught her bathing with his men in a stream.

THE CALAMITY JANE APOCRYPHA

There was a huge vested interest in creating Calamity

Jane, and that's why so much pure fiction about her has been willingly transformed into fact.

Thanks to the telegraph and the Associated Press (founded in 1840s), "Wild West" adventures had become breakfast-table fare for millions. Calamity Jane didn't matter as a person; she was a broad type, a "frontier character." So much so that Bret Harte is reported to have based his famous character Cherokee Sal on Jane.

By no means was Jane the first or only pistol-packin' mama on the frontier. There was Belle Starr, "a swaggerer with a six-gun on either ample hip." And there were two bootleggers turned rustler, Cattle Annie McDougall and Little Britches (Jennie) Metcalf. But Calamity's is the name that has endured, not so much because of any actual deeds but because of her remarkable ability to play to type and a hero-hungry media more interested in a "terrific sensation" than the facts themselves.

For example, there's a life-size replica of Calamity Jane in the Gunfighter's Wax Museum in Dodge City, right across the street from the town's famous old

Boot-Hill Cemetery. Calamity is also routinely included in literary collections about famous gunfighters.

Only one little problem: There's no proof she was ever a gunfighter. Perhaps the myth got started with stories like this news item from the June 23, 1898, Klondike Nugget, when Calamity Jane visited Dawson: " . . . on more than one occasion she has been forced to take human life in defense of her own." And while by all accounts she was a crack shot, and she certainly did like to fire off those Colt .45s of hers, she spent her time shooting out gaslights and mirrors behind bars. She did pal around with gunslingers like Arkansas Tom, and she did spend a lot of time in jails and stockades, but usually for drunkenness, lewdness, or just disturbing the peace.

Hell, that's chicken fixens. A gunfighter gets charged with murder, by God. And he's supposed to "buck out in smoke" (die in a gun battle), not "expire" of inflamed bowels and pneumonia in a hotel room. Where was her OK Corral, her high noon showdown in Abilene or Dodge? How many vigilante "hemp committees" (hangings) did she escape "in a hail of blue whistlers"? Where, in fact, is the proof she ever even killed anyone?

Calamity was a ripsnorter, true, a heller, a drinker, a fornicator—in other words, she was one of the guys (most men accepted Jane and liked her; it was her own sex that snubbed and rejected her). But she was not a gunfighter. That honorific was bestowed upon her by the mythmakers.

As was the title "military scout." Many sources mention, in one sentence, that Calamity Jane "found employment as a bullwhacker and scout." There's ample proof of the bullwhacking, none for the scouting. Jane was either drunk when she made that claim, or she was slyly building her legacy, or perhaps both. Not only is there no paper trail to verify she was ever paid for scouting, her details (dates, etc.) have been thoroughly discredited.

Much of the basis for Calamity Jane's scouting claim comes from the following passage from Life and Adventures of Calamity Jane: "I had a great many adventures with the Indians, for as a scout I had a great many dangerous missions to perform and while I was in many close places always succeeded in getting away safely for by this time I was considered the most reckless and daring rider and one of the best shots in the western country." It's Jane's say-so alone.

Calamity Jane claimed to have been married, as stated earlier, but no marriage licenses can be found; she also claimed to have a daughter, but there's no birth certificate. And it was only after Wild Bill had "gone over the range" and couldn't ever contradict her that she claimed they'd been lovers. Hollywood has made plenty of hay out of this unlikely romance over the years. And yet even as late as 1896, when her little 25-cent pamphlet appeared, she erroneously referred to Wild Bill as "Wm. Hickok." His name was James Butler; "Bill" was only a nickname.

Perhaps it was the ghostwriter's fault. Yet incredibly, given all the publicity about Hickok's death, Jane even got the name of the saloon where he died wrong, noting that he was shot "while setting [sic] at a gambling table in the Bell Union saloon."

Even if Calamity Jane snookered history, most of

her "stretches" were probably innocent enough. After all, "bullshitting the pilgrims" is not the same as lying. Her whoppers no doubt were mostly to entertain and keep drinks coming.

THE MANY FACES OF CALAMITY

In 1871, before the House Judiciary Committee, Victoria Woodhull, the first woman to testify before Congress, advocated for women's suffrage and "free love" outside of marriage. But Calamity Jane didn't give a damn about any high-toned society bitch—she had been dispensing free love for years and violating every other sanction that supposedly governed women.

This free spirit was a true pioneer in the arena of women's rights—no "lady-broke" horses for her. And yet, traditionally, Hollywood simply cashed in on the name value of Calamity Jane and ignored the real woman behind the myth, creating their own sanitized, baby doll versions of Jane. Doris Day, Yvonne De Carlo, Jane Russell, Jean Arthur, Ellen Barkin: casting directors have shown a decided preference for gossamer blond Janes.

Which poses a real challenge for David Milch and his writers as they try to reinvent Calamity Jane (Robin Weigert) in a way that brings her to life, not caricature. They have settled on an acerbic, combative, alcoholic, emotionally disturbed Jane who is occasionally quite funny but more often than not even unhappy and pathetic.

Weigert is convincing in the role, and her interpretation of Jane brings some humanity to what's become a meaningless stereotype. However, her take on Jane may be more faithful to her later life, when alcoholism had wreaked havoc on her personality and she had sunk into chronic depression. During the early years in Deadwood, the real Calamity Jane seems not to have been as antisocial and dysfunctional as Weigert's interpretation.

In fact, Jane was the life of the honky-tonks in Deadwood Gulch. Calamity practically lived—no, reigned—in Al Swearengen's Gem, where the bartenders knew her line when she bellied up: "Give me a shot of booze and slop it over the brim."

Apparently, she had a hair-trigger temper and could instantly get "mad as a peeled rattler," nor was she shy about brandishing her Colt .45s. But then she was all smiles when the miscreant bought her a drink.

Jane was a "chawer," too, and she could spit tobacco with the best of them. And when "the itch" was on her, which it was often, she'd "go off into the brush" with the first man she could find who didn't charge a stud fee. It's possible, based on the time she spent in whorehouses, that she even worked as a prostitute now and then when her pockets got light. The record shows, however, that she was only a laborer in houses of ill repute. In other words, she worked on the beds, not in them.

Without question, Calamity Jane was well liked and popular. She was recognized everywhere, and the moment she slapped open the bat wing saloon doors, the same shout always rang out: "Here comes Calamity Jane!" Maybe it was a warning, not a greeting—she was fond of "shooting down chandeliers," after all, whether anyone was sitting under them or not.

Obviously, "John Law" wasn't always so amused by

Jane's antics as the newspapers were, especially when she was hopped up on tarantula juice. But the best way to remember Calamity Jane is the way that Deadwood chooses to remember her: as a heroine. Like her friend Dora DuFran, she put her life on the line for Deadwood's residents. Maybe she never faced a showdown in Tombstone, but some might argue it takes more courage to risk a slow death from smallpox than a quick death from a bullet.

Calamity Jane's hoodwinking of a willing press and public is funny and admirable, not scandalous. Who can blame her for taking what was offered? She was one of the first masters of "spin" and of image control. Even today, naive writers report her manufactured stories as fact, never realizing they have been had by the best in the West—Calamity Jane, gold camp nurse and bullshit artist extraordinaire. And while she may have dressed like a man, here was a woman indeed.

CHAPTER TEN

"THE DEATH HUG'S A-COMIN'": WILD BILL HICKOK

I n the summer of 1865, the Hollywood Western was born in Springfield, Missouri. And Wild Bill Hickok was the somewhat bemused father, with plenty of help from a fawning press.

Prowling the streets and town square, adrenaline and testosterone rising, Hickok and an acquaintance named Dave Tutt kept a wary eye on each other as they "nerved up," then finally closed in for the kill. It was not planned, simply the consequence of Tutt's having insulted Hickok as Tutt was on his way out of a gambling establishment in Springfield (a blonde, a gambling debt, and Hickok's purloined watch were in the mix).

When Hickok followed him out a couple minutes later, it may have been to kill him, but not in a walk-

and-draw shootout in the street (which became a staple climax of the Western for most of the twentieth century)—that bit of drama was about to be born, and with a literal twist.

The two men edged closer to each other, drawing a crowd. Re-creations of the fight show Tutt slapping leather first, but it was the ambidextrous Hickok who scored the first hit. The gunfighters who prevailed repeatedly, as Hickok did, never forgot that "the first shot was often the only shot." Several witnesses of Hickok in action emphasized his remarkable ability to stay cool and take very careful aim.

But what added even more mystique to that now famous first walking showdown was Bill's reaction. Knowing Tutt had friends to back him up (or try to avenge him as the case may have been), in the blink of an eye after firing the fatal shot, Hickok immediately spun around, crouched with still-smoking gun leveled at the spectators, and asked if anyone else wanted a taste of the same.

The locals were outraged, Hickok was arrested (and later beat the rap), but it was all a lark to a sensation-hungry Civil War Union colonel named George W. Nichols, who edited the popular Harper's New Monthly Magazine. He met Hickok and no doubt for good reason was in awe of him. He transformed the flamboyant Wild Bill's adventures, including the Missouri shootout, into epic-heroic myth way bigger than life, even comparing Hickok to both Samson and Hercules.

In defense of the colonel's hyperbole, viewing Wild Bill Hickok really did seem to have a profound effect on both sexes. Custer, who deferred to few men, was visibly impressed by the figure Wild Bill cut. Custer's wife, Libbie, deeply in love with her dashing and famous soldier husband, nonetheless confessed, "I do not recall anything finer in the way of physical perfection than Wild Bill." Ellis Pierce, the Deadwood Gulch doc who helped Colorado Charlie wash the blood from the dead Hickok's hair, said, "Wild Bill was the prettiest corpse I have ever seen."

Hickok, a bit of a dandy, took pains to look striking, but he would come to regret that he had ever courted fame.

Wild Bill Hickok, from a photograph taken in New York, 1873. Courtesy of The Adams Museum & House, Deadwood, South Dakota.

AS THE TWIG IS BENT ...

Wild Bill Hickok has been described as a "natural loner," and one reason he sought solitude was so he could relax from the constant vigilance his notoriety required when he was around people. Hickok's fame was inescapable, and there were a lot of unstable types eager for some recognition themselves. That threat only increased after a rumor was floated that a family in Texas would pay $10,000 to Hickok's killer, to avenge their cowboy son who was killed by Hickok. This rumor might have been planted by Texas cowboys sick of Wild Bill's heavy hand while he was the law in Abilene and Hays City.

Notoriety like this, coupled with the showy name and those two ivory-gripped Colt Navys jammed butt forward in a scarlet sash), ensure that Wild Bill would remain a "gunfighter," a bad boy. But there were blatantly criminal gunfighters like Jesse James and John Wesley Hardin ("I take no sass but sassparilla"), and lawman-gunfighters like Hickok and Earp. Some revisionist historians seem eager to blur that distinction, but in Hickok's case, at least, the line is clear.

"He never wantonly took human life," eulogized his friend Captain Jack Crawford, ". . . there is no instance on record where he shed blood except in defence of his own life or in the line of duty as a peace officer."

Young Hickok's strong sense of right and wrong was learned in action, not abstraction. Born in 1837 in Troy Grove, Illinois, James Butler Hickok is a descendent of Francis Cooke, a member of the landing party that disembarked from the Mayflower in 1620. Hickok's parents were farmers and abolitionists—in fact, their home was a stop on the Underground Railway. Hickok took an active hand in "hiding and helping runaway slaves." Early on, he learned to see a sharp distinction between right and wrong—and to take action to correct wrongs.

While still a boy, James bought a pistol with money he earned and began practicing marksmanship behind the barn. He was ambidextrous and wisely practiced with each hand, giving himself a decided edge for later gun battles. Incredibly, he became "Marshal Hickok" by age fourteen or fifteen, for

Monticello Township, Illinois.

Spy, scout, soldier, detective, lawman, gambler, showman—Wild Bill would fill many roles in his thirty-nine years. He made his way west, and, like Buffalo Bill, rode for the oft-romanticized, ill-fated Pony Express. But while a stagecoach driver on the Santa Fe Trail, Bill was so severely mauled by a grizzly it nearly ended his career. The tough young frontiersman recovered, however, and the company sent him next to Rock Creek Station, Nebraska, where his reputation as a gunfighter was born in July 1861.

The story has been wildly exaggerated, with Hickok killing "six or seven men," and the details are still in dispute. A fellow named McCanles, former owner of Rock Creek Station, tried to take it back by force from the new owners. Hickok sided with the new owners, and when the fight was over three men lay dead, McCanles among them. It's not even known if Hickok killed him, but he got the notch for it.

But the moniker "Wild Bill" had not yet been bestowed—it's assumed Hickok earned that somewhat puzzling name during the Civil War "from fellow scouts and soldiers for his courageous acts against Confederate guerrillas and bushwhackers." He joined the Union Army as a teamster, eventually serving as a sharpshooter, scout, and spy.

Some of the impetus for the name could be the fact that Hickok was captured three times by the Rebels and escaped hanging each time at the eleventh hour. His extraordinary luck eventually became legendary, with people sometimes approaching him and politely asking, "Touch you for luck, Wild Bill?"

During the postbellum Indian campaigns, Hickok was a scout for Custer and his 7th Cavalry. In March 1867, a cavalry unit in Wyoming included "Wild Bill Hickok fashionably attired in a jacket of many colors and a ten gallon hat, his luxuriant mustachios flowing in the prairie breeze." It was then that he enjoyed his greatest fame—as a lawman cleaning up frontier hellholes no one else could tame. Places like Hays City, Kansas, a cow town mare's nest with "22 saloons and one grocery." But it was in Abilene, first among fabled cow towns, that his reputation finally became too dangerous to live with.

"Sure glad to see you," Marshal Hickok would greet the cowboys. "But hand over those guns."

Bill packed a star in Abilene in 1871, the town's busiest cattle season. Yet, with all that cash changing hands, during the nine months Wild Bill was the law there wasn't one holdup. Unfortunately, one night he had a shootout with Phil Coe, co-owner of Abilene's (in)famous Bull's Head Saloon. A heel scraped behind him, Hickok did his whirl-and-fire trick, and in the grainy twilight he killed his own deputy.

Many think Hickok was losing his eyesight by this time. Records in the National Archives prove he later visited the post physician in Cheyenne, who noted the patient was "going blind from glaucoma." Killing his own deputy seems to have soured Wild Bill on law enforcement. The final phase of his life begins: an unsuccessful stint with Bill Cody's Theatrical Troupe (Bill, a man of action, couldn't act worth a damn); bouts of gambling; and, on March 5, 1876, his marriage to Agnes Lake Thatcher, a circus owner and performer.

But as soon as the honeymoon was over, Wild Bill

joined Charlie Utter's wagon train bound for the gold-strike camp of Deadwood. He was married now and hoped to get rich so he could support his wife. And he was fully aware that his "mankiller" reputation had preceded him down the trail.

"I WON'T LEAVE IT ALIVE."

Wild Bill Hickok's arrival in Deadwood Gulch in July of 1876 no doubt caused more fanfare than he welcomed. The men of Deadwood had formed a parade to greet the whores traveling with Charlie Utter's train. By now, Wild Bill was the most famous man in the West, perhaps in America. No wonder he felt a premonition of his own death. In front of witnesses, he told Utter: "Charlie, I feel this is going to be my last camp, and I won't leave it alive." Even more convincing, because it's dated, is a letter to his wife the day before he was killed: ". . . if such should be we never meet again, while firing my last shot, I will gently breathe the name of my wife."

Deadwood's Wild Bill (played by Keith Carradine) stayed in a hotel; in reality Hickok stayed at Charlie

Utter's camp. Thadd Turner offers a possible reason he favored Mann, Lewis, and Nuttall's No. 10 Saloon: "Located on the lower end of Deadwood City's rapidly growing Main Street, this simple, rough-sawed wood structure was easily accessed from Charlie Utter's camp across Whitewood Creek and enabled Bill to avoid unwanted exposure on the heaviest part of the bustling street."

Many myths surround the death of Wild Bill, including the famous "dead man's hand" (it's not known what cards Hickok was holding at his death). But there's no mystery about who killed him on August 2, 1876, in the No. 10 Saloon—a twenty-five-year-old miner named John "Jack" McCall, who went by the alias Bill Sutherland. However, the why still stirs up debate.

Three possibilities stand out: 1. Jack McCall wanted the notoriety of killing someone as famous as Hickok; 2. McCall was motivated by the rumored $10,000 reward to Hickok's killer; 3. McCall was paid (as he claimed at his second trial) by a criminal faction in Deadwood who wanted Hickok dead. After all, Wild

Bill Hickok had a reputation for being a crusader who "cleaned towns up." And not even three weeks after McCall literally blew Hickok's brains out, Deadwood's only other "moral force," Preacher Smith, was murdered.

Writers have lamented that Wild Bill died a tragic death, that his life was cut tragically short. Butby age thirty-nine, Hickok had lived a fairly long life by gunfighter standards (any man who reached forty was considered old in those days). Since he was probably going blind (in addition to several other serious ailments), and given who and what he was, the blunt truth is that Hickok's end was fairly merciful—he never saw it coming, as the phrase goes.

Wild Bill Hickok died on the cusp of modernity. New inventions, between the year of his death and that of Calamity Jane's in 1903, included the telephone, the electric light, the phonograph, the gas engine, inoculation, stereophonic sound, the motorcar, the steam turbine, the motorcycle, the X ray, the diesel engine, the radio, the teleprinter, and the tape recorder. The "Old West" died in those thirty years, and a man like Hickok belonged to the Old West.

What tragedy? Wild Bill Hickok led a full life and left anindelible mark. His courageous actions gave rise to the single greatest moment in hundreds of Westerns—the walk-and-draw shootout. More important, Wild Bill was the first, and greatest, of all the gunfighters.

CHAPTER ELEVEN

AFTER THE BOOM:
AT PEACE ON MT. MORIAH

Special places get special recognition. Since 1917, and with congressional permission, the U.S. flag has flown night and day at Mt. Moriah Cemetery, Deadwood's famous, and recently restored, boot hill.

The cemetery, established between 1877 and 1878, occupies a steep hill above the town, and over the years the growth of trees has blocked some of its earlier, spectacular views. But many of the 3,627 people (according to the City of Deadwood web site) known to be buried there were Black Hills pioneers, including some Chinese, although most left requests to eventually be reburied in China.

The impressive roll call of the dead buried on Mt. Moriah includes many of the individuals discussed in

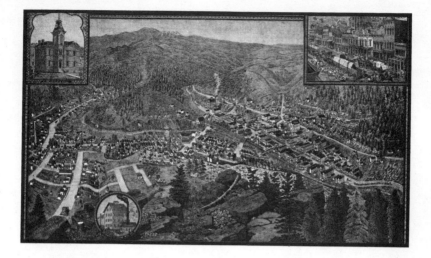

Map of Deadwood, 1884. Insets: Deadwood public school (top left), Deadwood street scene (top right), Deadwood Flouring Mill Co. (bottom). (Denver Public Library, Western History Collection, CG4184.D4 1884.H4).

this book—names that are becoming more familiar to those outside the Black Hills as interest in early Deadwood grows:

W. E. Adams died of a stroke in 1934, leaving behind the largest estate to ever go through probate in South Dakota. His second wife, Mary, survived him by almost sixty years. Mary's philanthropic efforts have preserved the Adams House Museum and benefited Deadwood Hospital and other organizations. They are both buried in California.

Outlaw Sam Bass, "Robin Hood on a Fast Horse," died in Round Rock, Texas, on his twenty-seventh birthday, mortally wounded by a Texas Ranger. Jim "Judas" Murphy, the gang member who ratted him out, committed suicide a year later, so great was his fear of the mythical "Sam Bass's Army."

Seth Bullock died in room 211 of his own hotel in 1919 at the age of seventy. Even while dying, he dedicated himself to a final public project: the first memorial to Theodore Roosevelt in the United States. That's why Bullock was buried 750 feet above the main part of Mt. Moriah, so that the nearby Mt. Roosevelt memorial would be visible. Pines block it today.

Calamity Jane died in the Calloway Hotel in the small mining town of Terry, South Dakota, from complications due to alcohol poisoning. Her funeral in Deadwood was the largest ever held for a woman. It's reported that her coffin was closed by a man who, as a boy, Jane saved from smallpox. There's no proof she ever requested to be buried next to Wild Bill, but that's where the world can find her.

Buffalo Bill Cody's Wild West Show went bankrupt

in 1913. Four years later, "the most famous man in America" died in Denver and was later buried on Lookout Mountain, Colorado.

Crazy Horse was arrested on September 5, 1877, amid rumors he planned a return to battle. While an Indian guard held his arms, a soldier killed him with the thrust of a bayonet. No one knows for sure where his remains are. In the Black Hills, near Gutzon Borglum's Mount Rushmore National Monument, sculptors are carving a massive statue of Crazy Horse from a mountain of granite six hundred feet high.

Dora DuFran "never missed a Days of '76 celebration," but she died on August 5, just missing the 1934 celebration. She's in Mt. Moriah "with her pet parrot Fred at her feet."

Wyatt Earp, unlike Hickok and so many other gunfighting legends, died with his boots off in 1929 in Los Angeles at the venerable age of eighty-one. Former cowboy turned Western star Tom Mix served as a pallbearer. He wept openly.

Wild Bill Hickok's grave remains the centerpiece at Mt. Moriah Cemetery. More than a hundred thousand faithful visit it annually. A graveside ceremony slated for August 2004 will induct Wild Bill posthumously into the Sons of the American Revolution.

"Poker Alice" Ivers died in Rapid City on February 27, 1930. She's buried in St. Aloysis Cemetery in the Black Hills.

Nat Love ("Deadwood Dick") eventually gave up rodeos and cattle nursing and became a Pullman car porter instead.

Jack McCall was hanged in Yankton, Dakota Territory, in March 1877–and buried there with the noose still around his neck.

"Potato Creek" Johnny died in February 1943 at the age of seventy-seven in Deadwood. He, too, occupies a place of honor in Mt. Moriah.

Theodore Roosevelt, the cowboy president whose Dakota days were the cornerstone of his rugged manhood, died in January 1919, only nine months before his good friend Seth Bullock.

Preacher Smith (Reverend H. W. Smith) has been proudly adopted by Deadwood and rests in Mt. Moriah

Steve and Charlie Utter at Hickok's first grave site. Courtesy of The Adams Museum & House, Deadwood, South Dakota.

Cemetery. The city rededicated a monument to this "earnest worker in his Master's Vineyard," as Bullock called him. The ceremony included the reading of the sermon he never got to deliver.

Doctor Flora Hayward Stanford went on to homestead in Wyoming, where she ran her own Double-D ranch. She died at age sixty-two and is buried in Mt. Moriah.

Sol Star, Seth Bullock's lifelong partner, died on

October 10, 1917. He was buried in St. Louis.

Al Swearengen, despite the Gem's success, died broke. He left Deadwood after the 1899 fire and was killed in Denver trying to hop a train. In response to a growing number of queries, the Adams Museum has hired a part-time archivist to find out more information about Swearengen and other less famous people from old Deadwood.

"Colorado" Charlie Utter became a man of mystery, his fate and date of death unknown except that after the turn of the century, he was rumored to have become "an American Indian doctor" in Panama.

As for Deadwood's former Chinatown—or at least some of it—it's being "exhumed." Deadwood Magazine reports the city has funded an archaeological dig on lower Main Street that has already yielded more than seventy-five thousand artifacts, ranging from opium pipes to glazed porcelain. In the early 1990s, Deadwood revived its tradition of a "colorful Chinese New Year celebration."

After their great victory at Little Bighorn, the Lakota were forced to cede the Black Hills and accept a smaller reservation. Today, the hills are still mined for gold, corporations having moved in after the surface deposits were gone. But the industry is not the major employer it once was, especially with the closing of the Homestake Mine in Lead. Logging remains important, and it's no surprise tourism is brisk in the warmer months. Why not, with all the wildlife and the quiet ghost towns located "back of beyond" in the historic hills?

And although hostilities have ceased, not all of the sixty-two thousand American Indians who live in South Dakota today, most of them Lakota or related tribes, have quit claim to the Paha Sapa. The legal battle over the 1868 Ft. Laramie Treaty continues.

BOOMTOWN TO COUNTY SEAT

Deadwood, too, could have become a ghost town by now. Several times. But like Tombstone, it's a town too tough to die.

Deadwood Gulch is no stranger to disaster. The first was the great fire of '79, which broke out in a bakery on Sherman Street and quickly gutted the business district. Not quite four years later, a flood, triggered by spring snowstorms. washed away most of Deadwood. A year later, "Demon Flame" struck yet again, this one starting in a boardinghouse, and once again destroying the business district.

That fire is why the Deadwood of today is Victorian brick: the building code was finally changed. Even so, another fire in 1952 destroyed City Hall and its wealth of archives. Other big fires, in 1959 and 2002, were contained by some impressive firefighting efforts. But Deadwood's history since 1876 has embraced much more than just disasters.

The 1880s saw the development of a thriving Chinatown that would endure into the 1920s, and by 1891 Deadwood had a railroad link to the outside world—a real sign the boomtown was becoming a community. The Prohibition Act of 1919 fired up reformers to go after gambling and prostitution in Deadwood, but in the true frontier spirit both still flourished illegally. With the repeal of Prohibition in 1935, gambling went great guns until it ended officially in 1947. During the '50s and '60s, the state's attorney shut down most of the brothels in Deadwood as well.

In 1964, the entire city of Deadwood was designated a National Historic Landmark—the first community so honored. In 1980, Pam's Purple Door, the last brothel, closed for business. Then legalized gambling in Deadwood was approved by South Dakota voters in 1988, and the timing was good: only nine years later, serious layoffs began at the Homestake. Some eighty casinos now operate in the Gulch, offering from nickel slots to $100 bet limits.

The return of wagering to Deadwood has created a second boom, especially as much of the revenue funds historical preservation. But there's also been a joke going around since gaming returned about how lawyers have raised more buildings in Deadwood than contractors have.

It seems that South Dakota state law limits the number of gaming devices (slot machines, etc.) to "30 per building." That has led to some creative decisions by the gaming board as to what constitutes a "building," reported Scott Randolph in the April 13, 2004, issue of the Black Hills Pioneer. Decisions that might leave most building inspectors astounded. Such as a recent ruling that a casino was actually two "buildings" because ground radar showed fragments of old foundations under the casino!

This suggests that some elements of frontier Deadwood still prevail. Nor should it be otherwise in a town so in tune with its past. But there's far more than slots and blackjack to recommend this picturesque Old West mining town. There's an old gold mine where visitors can pan for gold, and plenty of historic saloons and hotels—restored, of course, but many on the same sites where Wild Bill, Calamity Jane, Seth Bullock, and many others frequented them. (You may even spot the apparition of Seth Bullock if you stay in his hotel, but rest easy: Seth was decent, and so is his spirit, which reportedly helped a lost child back to his room.)

Mt. Moriah Cemetery draws international visitors all by itself. There's also several historical museums, including the Adams Museum in the heart of Deadwood on Sherman Street, the first history museum in the Black Hills. It was built by W. E. Adams in 1930 to both memorialize his family and honor the area's other early pioneers. The Adams Home, a Victorian mansion built in 1892, became the Adams House Museum at 22 Van Buren Street.

As for how real Deadwood residents feel about the HBO series: on the edge of town, prominently situated, workers are recreating *Deadwood*'s favorite watering hole—the Gem shall one day soon pour drinks again.

And, of course, since one specific event has linked Wild Bill Hickok to Deadwood forever, in the summers visitors can watch Wild Bill get shot four times a day at the Old Style Saloon No. 10. The reenactment is free of charge and stars James West of Cody, Wyoming. And every evening except Sunday, deputies chase "Jack McCall" and capture him on historic Main Street, then hustle him off to trial. The public is definitely invited.

BOOKS AND WEB SITES FOR FURTHER READING

BOOKS

Bennett, Estelline. *Old Deadwood Days*. Narrative Press, 2001.

Dexter, Pete. *Deadwood* (novel). Penguin, 1986.

Estleman, Loren D. *Aces & Eights* (novel). Doubleday, 1981.

Flexner, James. *Doctors on Horseback*. Viking Press, 1937.

Frazier, Ian. *Great Plains*. Penguin, 1989.

Lavender, David. *The Great West*. Houghton Mifflin, 1965.

McCutcheon, Marc. *The Writer's Guide to Everyday Life in the 1800s*. Writer's Digest Books, 1993.

McClintock, John S. *Pioneer Days in the Black Hills*. University of Oklahoma Press, 2000.

McMurtry, Larry. *Buffalo Girls* (a novel about Dora DuFran and Calamity Jane). Simon & Schuster, 2001.

Parker, Watson. *Gold in the Black Hills*. University of Oklahoma Press, 1966.

Webb, Walter Prescott. *The Great Plains*. Grosset & Dunlap, 1931.

WEB SITES ABOUT CONTEMPORARY AND HISTORIC DEADWOOD
Adams Museum and House:www.adamsmuseumandhouse.org
City of Deadwood: www.cityofdcadwood.com
Deadwood Magazine: www.deadwoodmagazine.com

OTHER SITES DEVOTED TO DEADWOOD
www.deadwood.net
www.deadwood.org
www.deadwooddiscovered.com
www.deadwoodunderground.com
www.heartofdeadwood.com
www.historicdeadwood.com

WEB SITES ABOUT THE BLACK HILLS
Rapid City Journal: www.rapidcityjournal.com
www.theblackhills.com
www.rapidweb.com

WEB SITES ABOUT SOUTH DAKOTA
South Dakota State Historical Society: www.sdhistory.org
Travel in South Dakota: www.ravelsd.com

TELEVISION
HBO's *Deadwood*: www.hbo.com

John Edward Ames has an MA in English and taught writing at the University of Northern Colorado and University of New Mexico before becoming a full time writer in 1987. His 56 novels include 45 westerns and western historicals. *The Unwritten Order* (1995) was nominated for a Spur Award from the Western Writers of America. He began his writing career at age 19 as a journalist in the U. S. Marine Corps.